shop london

...

GW00640789

Siân Tichar
Photographs by Maria Satur

shop london

a guide

• • • ellipsis

•••

All rights reserved. No part of this publication may be reproduced in any form without written permission from the publisher

BRITISH LIBRARY CATALOGUING IN PUBLICATION
A CIP record for this book is available from the British Library

PUBLISHED BY •••ellipsis
2 Rufus Street London N1 6PE
WWW http://www.ellipsis.com
SERIES EDITOR Tom Neville

COPYRIGHT © 2000 Ellipsis London Limited
ISBN 1 84166 032 9

PRINTING AND BINDING Hong Kong

•••ellipsis is a trademark of Ellipsis London Limited

For a copy of the Ellipsis catalogue or information on special quantity orders of Ellipsis books please contact
Faye Chang
020 7739 3157 or faye@ellipsis.co.uk

Siân Tichar 2000

contents

Introduction

England is one of the most successful and adaptable retailing countries in the world and London has long been one of the main destinations for international shoppers. But, like the megalopoli of New York and Paris, its scale and diversity can leave even the most hardened shopper feeling that they've overdosed on retail therapy. *Shop London* is an overview that is designed to prevent over-indulgence by careful selection.

Shopping is the most popular leisure activity in the United Kingdom. This fact is self perpetuating because the more people shop, the more shops open to accommodate them. More importantly, the shops that already exist have adapted to meet the needs of their customers. Shops are no longer places that we simply enter, purchase something and leave. The whole experience is now a highly developed activity. Owners of shops – from boutique to department store – actively encourage consumers to spend time in their premises. In the large-scale stores this is achieved by displaying vast ranges of merchandise that can take customers hours to peruse, and providing bars, cafés and restaurants where refreshment can be had without the consumer ever having to leave the place. On a smaller scale, shops are stocking high-quality design-based goods which customers should take time to examine and understand.

Of course, the idea that shopping has become more than just about purchasing products is not so applicable in the case of indigenous high-street chain shops and brands. This is apparent from the fact that Selfridges is the only shop on Oxford Street (Britain's ultimate high street) featured in this book. Shopping presented as a lifestyle experience was one of the main criteria for stores to be included in *Shop London*. London has so many wonderful shops that meet a diverse range of needs that when the original site list for the book was drawn up it was in danger of becoming a never-ending number of visit-worthy shops. To avoid this, entry criteria had to be defined more exclusively. Unusualness, inspirational quality and, most importantly, design-consciousness became the definitive factors. Some of the obvious international brand names could immediately be discounted. Prada, Miu Miu and Calvin Klein have very beautiful and very design-conscious shops but they stock the same items, in similarly designed spaces, in every major city of the world.

Shop London defined itself by including shops that cannot always be found in other cities and other countries. Yet there are some exceptions to this rule. Some international brands – Aveda, Donna Karan, Issey Miyake, Versace – made the grade simply because their products, sites or philosophies are just too inspirational not to be included. The ultimate reason for inclusion therefore came down to a store's unique attitude to stocking well-designed products in a well-designed space. Shops such as Paul Smith, Vivienne Westwood and Nicole Farhi are also big, internationally recognised names and demanded inclusion both because they met the criteria but also because they are British. Their achievements in international markets have marked them out both in the United Kingdom and abroad, and their adaptability has been an essential factor in their success. Patrick Cox and Jo Malone qualified for these same reasons.

Some of the shops were included just because the stories around them are too good not to be shared. Mathmos and Planet Organic are wonderful examples of outlets where somebody with a good idea and incredible marketing skills has turned an obscurity into the mainstream. The people behind many of the shops are passionate about their products – whether they design or simply stock them – and consequently are interesting stories in themselves. Selina Blow, Lulu Guinness and Joe Corr (of Agent Provocateur), can all claim interesting family connections that add colour to the outlets and products that bear their names or for which they are responsible.

Introduction

A feature of the specialist boutique – whether it sells furniture, clothing, jewellery, bags or shoes – is that the stock is so recognisable that it becomes a kind of retail equivalent of a piece of art and the store takes on a similar role to that of a gallery. The relationship between shop and gallery, owner and dealer is explored in this book: examples include Mission, Space, Viaduct, Vessel and Mint. Here the sales team (more often than not these are the owners and founders) know the designers who supply their stock and encourage customers to spend time becoming familiar with their work. Some of these shops host exhibitions, displaying the work of the designers they sell and enhancing their careers at the same time. This expands the role of the owner from retailer to curator and allows the actual shop space to become multi-functional. The Oxo Tower has taken this idea to its limit by insisting that all the designers who rent space there also use their premises as a working studio.

This multi-functionalism is one of the most noticeable recent developments. Apart from providing exhibition space, even small shops are finding space for refreshments for customers. Aveda built a Love café and Viaduct and Sh! are happy to provide customers with tea or coffee while they look at the merchandise. Lulu Guinness went one step further and invented the Lulu Card, which entitles her regular customers to come in and relax, take tea or coffee, and a space to leave their bags whether they buy anything from her or not. Even the high-street chain stores are diversifying: Nike Town (at Oxford Circus), is a total experience with screens and video projections enhancing a visit; the Levi's Store (on Regent Street), employs in-house DJs. These adaptations are furthered by the late, and Sunday, opening hours of shops. London's multicultural influences helped bring about longer opening times – unheard of just ten years ago. Now furniture, clothes and luxury goods can be bought every day of the week, where once there were only mini-supermarkets catering for basic needs.

In fact London's shops cater for so much more than basic needs that many (and most of those in this book) have become temples to consumerism. The objects they display in architecturally astounding environments mean that people enjoy being in them whether they are there to purchase or merely to browse. Consumer goods are often lusted after as pornography might be. The idea of materialistic consumer pornography brings a whole new meaning to the standard assistant–customer conversation: 'Can I help you?' 'No, thank you, I'm just looking.'

Apart from the Oxo Tower, I have not ventured south of the Thames or far north of Islington. London is so vast that were I to have strayed from my west to east path *Shop London* would have had to take into account suburbs such as Richmond and Dulwich, and that the contents would have represented the sprawling growth of this capital. Instead – if you follow the chapters in order – you can travel on a fairly neat route through the inspiring design-conscious havens to which London is home.

ACKNOWLEDGEMENTS
I would like to thank the knowledge, expertise and extensive credit-card limits of Katia Hadidian and Rana Salam. Thanks to the Divine Miss C as well. Also a special thank you to Maria Satur. And to Tom Neville and Jonathan Moberly. Lastly, but not leastly, I would like to thank Liz and Karel Tichar. Also Julie, Sean, Shaune and David.

ST JUNE 2000

king's road

Designer's Guild

Trisha Guild is the aptly named woman behind this establishment interiors shop in the World's End section of the King's Road. Three shopfronts knocked together house a wide range of Guild's wallpapers, bedding, towels, sofas, glassware, ceramics and kitchenware. A patio garden on the lower ground level features plants and pots.

Guild has been a fixture on London's interiors scene for years. She – like Sir Terence Conran – is on the editorial board of *Elle Deco* magazine and has long been associated with making bold colour statements. More recently she has toned down her palette and started to use greys and pastels. Yet in some ways the Chelsea location and her clientele (Designer's Guild is popular with those who have the money to buy complete looks rather than come up with ideas themselves) have made Guild a rather predictable choice when it comes to home design.

ADDRESS 277 King's Road, London SW3 (020 7351 5775)
OPEN Monday to Tuesday, 9.30–17.30; Wednesday to Saturday, 10.00–19.00; Sunday, 12.00–17.00
UNDERGROUND Sloane Square

New King's Road Vintage Guitar Emporium

For guitar lovers, entering the New King's Road Vintage Guitar Emporium must be like having died and arrived in heaven, as the range of rare guitars for sale (I can't say 'on display' as the rarest remain safely tucked away in their cases at the rear of the store) is simply astounding. As are the prices which range from £400 to well over £40,000.

Rick Zsigmond – 'Fat Rick' to his friends – opened the shop in 1997 but has had guitar shops in London for 15 years. Zsigmond was originally a session drummer, but realised that there was more money to be made dealing in guitars and his mini Mecca was born. A recent coup was a Gibson 1958 Flying V. For those readers who don't know their Gibsons from their Fenders, this guitar is so rare that only two have passed through Zsigmond's outlets in the past fifteen years. Keith Richards played one at the Rolling Stones Hyde Park gig in June 1969 where he broke it on stage making, as Zsigmond points out, one less in the world from a total production of only 98.

The rare guitar market is very high-end in terms of cost, and this largely determines the kind of people who can afford to be active in it. Most of Zsigmond's customers (except for those from the music business) work in the City and are usually well into their thirties by the time they can afford to start collecting rare guitars seriously. The trend that led to the current value of vintage guitars really only began in the early 1980s. Many collectors are wise investors who also happen to love guitars. Simon Finch (see page 4.10) was a typical customer before he decided to come in with Zsigmond as a partner. They were joined by James Stevenson, who is the only working musician of the three. He has played with Billy Idol and Kim Wilde and is also forging a career as a producer.

The Emporium is a fascinating place to visit – you never know who

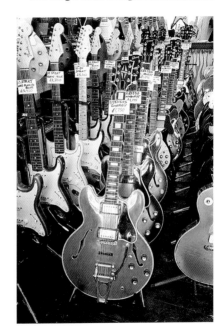

or what you will find there. Zsigmond sells guitars on behalf of some musicians as well and was proud to show a guitar that had belonged to the Stone Roses as well as a Gibson Les Paul Standard (1959) that has passed through the hands of both Jimmy Page and Dire Straits' Mark Knopfler during its 41-year existence. Zsigmond regularly produces a catalogue so that those on his mailing list remain aware of the specific guitars (and their individual history) in the shop at any given time.

The shop itself contains other rarities; the most impressive being its toilet wall. Over the years Zsigmond has had his famous customers sign this wall and anyone visiting the loo can see the scrawling of Holly Johnson (Frankie Goes to Hollywood), Mitch Mitchell (Jimi Hendrix Experience), Steve Jones and Glen Matlock (both Sex Pistols), Lloyd Grossman (a surprise vintage-guitar collector) and both the Gallagher brothers who are regular patrons. There are also signed pictures from most of the Rolling Stones and many other big music names.

In summer 2000 Zsigmond, Finch and Stevenson opened another shop in Denmark Street, London's main focus for guitar and music shops. But Zsigmond remains based on the King's Road. One suspects he does not like to stray from his increasingly impressive loo wall for too long.

ADDRESS 65a New King's Road, London SW6 (020 7371 0100)
WEBSITE www.newkingsroadguitars.co.uk
OPEN Monday to Saturday, 10.00–19.00
UNDERGROUND Fulham Broadway

ADDRESS first floor, 25 Denmark Street, London WC2 (020 7836 8008)
OPEN Monday to Saturday, 10.00–18.00
UNDERGROUND Tottenham Court Road

sloane square and knightsbridge

Liza Bruce

Liza Bruce's design work is based on the fact that she believes – rightly or wrongly – that women are still very much dictated to by the men of the fashion world. With this idea in mind Bruce began designing swimwear in 1985. Her suits and accessory pieces employed flattering cuts and unusual dying methods producing both vibrant and faded effects. This provided her starting point: small, stretchy under wear that would form the basis – on any body form – for other clothing. She herself began to design other clothing about eight years ago.

The shop opened in March 1998 and is as eye-catching on Pont Street as a supermodel wearing one of her one-pieces. Designed by her artist husband Nicholas Alvis-Vega, it is, in the words of the man himself, 'euphorically modern, without embracing the current fad for minimalism that in Liza's and my opinion is the epitome of bad taste'.

Taking the simple idea of a colour chart, Alvis-Vega painted rectangles of colour on to sections of the shop wall. Aztec and Egyptian principles inspired the furniture and the total effect is striking, clean, and very, very future. Just like Bruce's work. You never know what you might find on display from day to day and Bruce is always willing to make pieces up to fit particular body shapes.

ADDRESS 9 Pont Street, London SW1 (020 7235 8423)
OPEN Monday to Saturday, 11.00–18.00
UNDERGROUND Knightsbridge

Patrick Cox

It was the launch of the Patrick Cox Wannabe collection for autumn/winter 1993–94 that meant that Cox would never again have to be a wannabe. The laid-back comfortable loafer-style shoe that he designed for that collection put his name in every major fashion magazine in the Western hemisphere and on every major media man and woman's feet.

Although he is British-based and trained, Cox was born in Canada in 1963. He arrived in the UK to attend the footwear-design course at Cordwainers Technical College and was still studying when his talents were recognised by Vivienne Westwood, for whom he designed shoes back in 1984. Cox continued to work with some of the more-established figures of the fashion industry (John Galliano, Anna Sui, Workers for Freedom, John Rocha, Katherine Hamnett) as he was building up his own company but the success of the Wannabe collection allowed him to expand rapidly and open the shop on Sloane Street. He had already been selling to the public out of Symons Street and had opened shops in New York and Paris when he threw the Sloane Street doors open in September 1995. He has since launched and developed a clothing line. His work is in the permanent collections of the Victoria & Albert Museum, the Australian National Gallery, and the FIT Museum in New York. Despite all this, it is dedication to comfort and function that has defined Cox's success. He carries this through all his footwear designs, crowning them with the ultimate in personal transport; a scooter that bears his name.

ADDRESS 129 Sloane Street, London SW1 (020 7730 8886)
OPEN Monday to Saturday, 10.00–18.00; Wednesday, 10.00–19.00
UNDERGROUND Sloane Square

Lulu Guinness

For a woman who designed her first briefcase in 1989, Lulu Guinness has done phenomenally well. Her handbags – she gave up on the brief-cases soon after she began – now sell all over the world as well as through the two London stores that bear her name. Guinness's first outlet was on Elizabeth Street with Selina Blow, but in 1996 she moved to premises at 66 Ledbury Road, w11, from where she and her team still operate.

Her bag designs are original and instantly recognisable. The most famous resembles a flower pot; a plain silk base underneath a lid bursting with brightly coloured silk flowers. Guinness has recently started to custom-make bags to match wedding dresses and designed a sweet range of mix-n-match hair accessories.

Like Selina Blow, Lulu Guinness's name gives away the fact that there is more to her than mere bag-designer done well. She married into the Guinness (beer) family and this undoubtedly ensured her some initial attention from society magazines such as *Tatler* and *Harpers and Queen*. Yet of course it was the unique designs that have carried her name in the hands of society girls ever since. That and perhaps the fact that a Lulu Guinness bag will also bring you a 'Lulu Card'. Those privileged enough to hold one (you are awarded one when you purchase a bag) get to deposit their shopping at either of the stores while they continue browsing the vicinity, and complimentary tea and coffee is served to them on comfy sofas as they rest their retail-therapy Blahnik/Prada/Choo clad feet.

ADDRESS 3 Ellis Street, London SW1 (020 7823 4828)
WEBSITE www.luluguinness.com
OPEN Monday to Saturday, 10.00–18.00
TUBE Sloane Square

Harrods Food Halls

Harrods is famous for being famous and for its as yet unbroken promise that it will deliver whatever its customers desire, providing their request is neither illegal nor obscene, and that the customer pays for the specialised service they receive.

Unlike most of London's department stores, Harrods started life as a grocer rather than a draper. This was in 1849, when Knightsbridge was little more than a village and Charles Henry Harrod was a tea wholesaler who saw that proximity to Buckingham and Kensington palaces was attracting wealthy property buyers to the area. Harrods originally sold only non-perishable goods such as tea, but under the supervision of Charles Harrod's son it began offering fruit and vegetables as well.

The first of the food halls, and still the most famous, – that selling meat, fish and poultry – was built in 1901. Royal Doulton produced the tiles for the walls and a magnificent frieze, designed by W J Neatby, now carries a preservation order. It sells an incredible range of meat, fish and poultry, brought in fresh every day. The butchers can provide entire freezer-fulls of cut meat if that is what the customer desires (and pays for). Parrot fish, squid, mackerel and monk fish sit next to lobsters, crabs, oysters, prawns and mussels, not to mention a complete choice of caviar on huge beds of ice and the daily catch that is reflected in a fresh fish wall display artistically created by the staff (and thrown away after closing time).

The patisserie hall, stocking teas and coffees and a wide choice of confectionery – was the next to open. It too was decorated in beautiful tiles, but they were long covered up and forgotten about and only recently rediscovered for general admiration. As with all the halls, the patisserie treats all its products with singular respect. Harrods sells tea in the same style that it sells fine wines. Teas from different gardens all over the world,

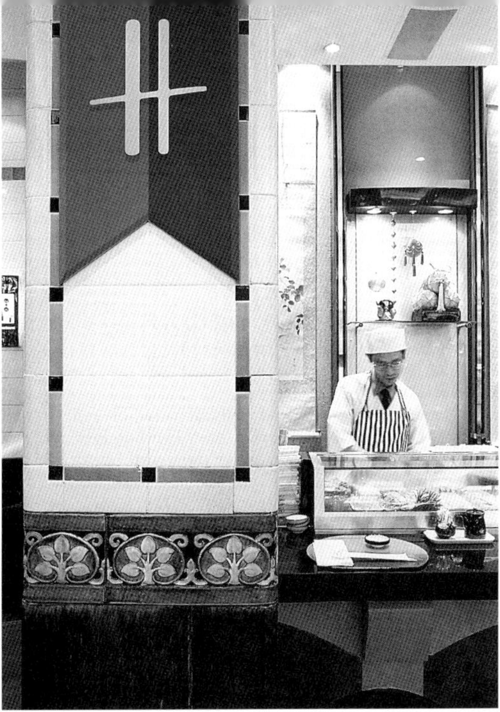

picked at different times of night and day to create different flavours, are all available. Coffee comes as beans or ground; organic, decaffeinated or flavoured. Confectionery includes Harrods own, as well as Swiss and Belgian varieties, and the delights of the patisserie counter are all produced downstairs in the huge kitchen that Mohamed Al-Fayed built after he purchased Harrods in 1985. The custom-made cakes can be as wild as your imagination providing they meet the three prerequisites. The largest to date was 6 feet long, 3 feet high, and modelled on an Arabian prince's castle. At the stroke of midnight, during the party for which the cake was made, seven white doves flew out from its centre.

The dairy and charcuterie hall houses an astounding 450 different cheeses and almost 100 types of bread. It is also the place to pick up ready-made food; a mouth-watering selection of exotic international dishes. Fruit and vegetables are flown in daily from all over the globe and are not so affected by seasonal changes. The candy hall was the first retail room to be opened by a member of the royal family when Princess Anne cut its inaugural ribbon in 1983. It sells sweets and is home to the bakery and leads down, via an escalator, to the pantry where supermarket products are sold. The wine department is also located in the basement and sells everything from Gordon's gin to bottles of claret at £4000.

Harrods really is one of London's most special stores and its food halls are the most special of its parts. Full of delightful surprises often at surprisingly affordable prices, the halls provide candy for the eye as well as the belly.

ADDRESS 87–135 Brompton Road, SW1 (020 7730 1234)
OPEN Monday, Saturday, 10.00–18.00; Tuesday to Friday, 10.00–19.00
UNDERGROUND Knightsbridge

Jo Malone

In 1983 at the age of twenty, after travelling to Grasse, the world centre of fragrance, Jo Malone began to practise her own technique for facial massage, using no electronic gadgetry or machines. A client list of 20 rapidly grew to 2000 and Malone dedicated herself to developing a skin-care line to meet the needs of both men and women.

The ingredients for her Juniper Skin Tonic and Vitamin E Gel were originally mixed in her kitchen with the help of husband and business partner Gary Wilcox. By 1994 Malone was ready to unleash her skincare and fragrance business on London and opened her first shop on Walton Street. She moved from there to the current 1200-square-foot site in 1999. A large skin-care bar displays open pots of her rich face creams that customers can sample. Fragrance booths (enter through a glass door and be blasted by whichever heady combinations of scents you desire) allow scents to be tested at the touch of a button and a lifestyle area displays the complete Jo Malone fragrance collection.

The reason that Malone's reputation has grown so quickly – her company has already been purchased by Estée Lauder – is that all her products smell divine and her creams and potions really work to help nurture skin. Her scented candles ensure that the homes of her disciples are wafted with nutmeg, ginger, cinnamon and citrus fruits. Tuberose, sandalwood, honeysuckle, lime blossom and jasmine are just some of the natural extracts she uses in a range of creams, potions, lotions and oils.

ADDRESS 150 Sloane Street, London SW1 (020 7730 2100)
WEBSITE www.jomalone.co.uk
OPEN Monday to Wednesday, Saturday, 10.00–18.00; Thursday, Friday 10.00–19.00
UNDERGROUND Sloane Square

FRAGRANCE
TESTING BOOTH

sloane square and knightsbridge

Basia Zarzycka

Stepping into Basia Zarzycka's boutique is like stepping into the eighteenth-century boudoir of a princess and her maids in waiting, full to the brim with tiaras spilling out of vases stuffed with flowers and feathers, jewel-encrusted brooches bursting from boxes lined in silk and smothered in ribbon – every bride's dream.

Of Polish descent, Zarzycka graduated from Goldsmiths' College having studied embroidery and textiles. An MA in fashion and constructed textiles from her home city of Birmingham set her up to design the unique fairy-tale gowns, tiaras and shoes for which she has become celebrated.

Wedding gowns with ballroom-style skirts swathed in organdie silk tulle and tight, breast-enhancing bodices embellished with hundreds of tiny Venetian beads and adorned with wild floral garlands have made her a sought-after designer. Zarzycka's range of more than 600 tiaras crafted from bijoux and natural freshwater pearls, delicate silk flowers and Austrian crystal has also brought her a lot of positive press. Combined with a pair of hand-made shoes crafted from beechwood and silk that matches the gown, there is no doubt that Zarzycka's work should not be worn by brides who blush, but rather those who wish to bloom.

ADDRESS 52 Sloane Square, London SW1 (020 7730 1660)
WEBSITE www.basia-zarzycka.co.uk
OPEN Monday to Saturday, 10.30–18.30
UNDERGROUND Sloane Square

brompton cross/
walton street

The Conran Shop

Founded by Sir Terence Conran – who also founded Habitat – The Conran Shop was opened on 19 November 1973 at 77 Fulham Road on the spot where his first Habitat had stood. It moved to its present location fourteen years later and has made dynamic use of the unique architectural masterpiece which is The Michelin Building.

The building, completed in 1911, was designed by Francois Espinasse for the Michelin Tyre Company. Although Espinasse was not a qualified architect (the only other building he is known to have designed is Michelin's Paris headquarters), he captured the spirit of the company's advertising campaign (based on the fat smiling man made of tyres) in The Michelin Building. Conran acquired it in 1987, and restored and redeveloped it. The effort has paid off – the remarkable building now houses the shop, the Bibendum oyster restaurant, and even some office space.

The Conran Shop has a diverse range of homewares, both contemporary and period pieces, displayed alongside the shop's own line of furniture and other items. The mix is eclectic and has featured pieces by Philippe Starck, Charles and Ray Eames, and Eileen Gray and a selection of fabric, rugs, bedlinen, cushions, lighting, glassware, stationary, vases, luggage, books, baskets, boxes and antiques. In case they missed anything, there are also a bathshop, kitchenshop and childshop. The fact that many of the pieces being sold now were stocked when the shop first opened stands as testimony to the skill of the buyers here.

ADDRESS 81 Fulham Road, London SW3 (020 7589 7401)
WEBSITE www.conran.co.uk
OPEN Monday, Tuesday, Friday, 10.00–18.00; Wednesday, Thursday, 10.00–19.00; Saturday, 10.00–18.30; Sunday, 12.00–18.00
UNDERGROUND South Kensington

Joseph

Brompton Cross, aka 'Joseph Junction', houses in close proximity the womenswear, menswear and Essentials shops of the Joseph fashion empire – and Joe's Café providing mid-shop sustenance. Moroccan-born Joseph Ettedgui, now in his 60s, switched from hairdressing to designing in the 1960s and recently sold his family-owned fashion house for a staggering £98.5 million.

Joseph's vision includes sexy trousers, incredibly smart suits, quality fabrics and glamorous evening wear alongside his famous knitwear lines. The clean and innovative style of his shops – more apparent at Brompton Cross than perhaps any other – reflect his clothes and the women who wear them. Brompton Cross has added pulling power, as it stocks Prada and other high-fashion labels alongside the fine Joseph pieces. Shop dressers make use of its huge space by creating innovative displays that are more about art than fashion and which change from season to season.

ADDRESS 77 Fulham Road, London SW3 (020 7823 9500)
OPEN Monday to Saturday, 10.00–18.30; Wednesday, 10.00–19.00; Sunday, 12.00–17.00
UNDERGROUND South Kensington

Voyage

Voyage set a shopping precedent when it closed its doors to the public in 1997. Six years after opening on the Fulham Road, husband and wife design team Tiziano and Louise Mazzilli were fed up with seeing their distinctive ideas on the catwalk and in the shops of other designers. They decided to put a stop to the spies and created a membership card for their 3000 or so core customers. What appears to be a rather ridiculous move in terms of sales and company growth makes perfect sense when seen in the context of Voyage's ethics.

The Mazzilli family consists of Italian Tiziano, Belgian Louise, and their two children, Tatum and Rocky. Tiziano and Louise worked successfully in the Italian fashion industry for 20 years alongside both Jean Franco Ferre and Cerrutti. They were behind the collections of Valentino but became tired with the way their work was diffused as it moved from drawing board to shopfloor. They invested all their savings in the then two-storey space at 115 Fulham Road and filled it with a hundred dresses. The first week went badly, but a brainwave from a former collection had them remove the dresses from the hangers, re-dye them and replace them as vibrant, distorted pieces. The result was phenomenal and Voyage was embedded in the fashion conscious via the glossy pages of international fashion magazines.

Now they spread their work over two shops. The pattern cutter and seamstresses who originally worked out of the basement at number 115 have moved to Battersea and a mezzanine has been added, giving the shop a first floor. Called Living In Voyage, it houses the women's couture collection and recently established lines of bags, shoes and lingerie. The Voyage Experience along the road at 175–177 Fulham Road is three storeys of mostly menswear, but with the basement given over to women's daywear and lingerie.

The shops were decorated by Tiziano and Louise. Warm wafts of incense fill the air of the stores and there is always an eclectic mix of music blaring from the stereo. Customers can take hours to work their way through each unique garment. Classic cuts with an eccentric twist and a brave, bold attitude to colour comprise the Voyage signature. Equally characteristic are the horrendous prices. Cardigans priced at £595, T-shirts at £295 and jackets at £1450 and rising also add to this store's exclusivity. Yet those who can afford to buy here – and Madonna, Cher and Tina Turner are among the celebrity membership-card holders – obviously delight in the fact that they can shop without being harassed by anyone other than the assistants.

Daughter Tatum is in charge of the shops and recently took control of the accessories and lingerie as well. Rocky is in charge of the press and marketing – it was he who was responsible for the advertising campaign that featured the family wearing their own clothes. They argue that, with four body shapes and ages, and both genders represented, they embody the consumers at whom they aim their stock. This egalitarian attitude is also apparent in sizing – one or two sizes will fit all.

Yet how egalitarian can a shop really be that sells clothes that can only be bought by the very wealthy and even then, only if they fit the criteria to get through the door in the first place? Critics of Voyage – and there are quite a few– say that it has cleverly marketed its image through hype without substance. Examination has proved that not all of the clothes are very well made and the one-size-fits-all is possible because none of the garments are cut to fit anyone; a sloppy, unprofessional attitude to tailoring and design alike. The music that you hear in the store is also available for sale, yet the discs are more expensive here than at the high-street music stores where Tiziano bought them. Voyage will argue that

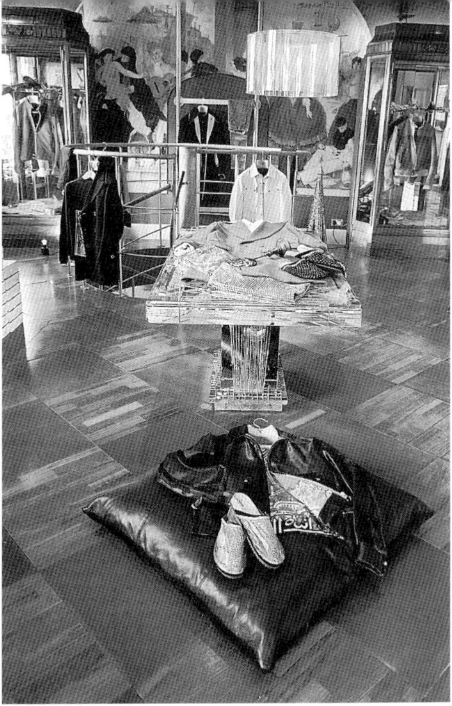

brompton cross/walton street

– like with the clothes pricing – you pay for something special (such as Tiziano's favourite CD or design of the moment): you are literally buying into the Voyage experience and living the Voyage life; and so it is worth it.

You can make up your own mind – if you can get into the shops.

ADDRESS 115 and 175–177 Fulham Road, London SW3 (020 7823 9581/ 020 7352 8611)
OPEN Monday to Friday, 10.30–18.30; Saturday, 10.30–18.00
UNDERGROUND South Kensington

Whistles

Twelve shops and 15 concessions mean that Whistles is a brand name recognised all over the United Kingdom. However, unlike many chain stores, it has maintained an individuality that often goes beyond trend and fashion.

The first Whistles was opened by South-African-born Lucille Lewin and her husband Richard in 1976 in a small shop on George Street, close to the current flagship store on St Christopher's Place. But it is the branch on Brompton Road that really exemplifies what Whistles is all about. More a boutique than a shop, it is crammed full of the bags, hats and accessories that Lewin loves to promote alongside the clothes.

'I design feminine clothes for girls and women', she says. 'And I don't think that women should be invisible in their clothes'. She uses textured fabrics in vibrant colours, adorning them with beads in unusual designs. Yet Lewin has only been designing her own line since 1989. Prior to that she stocked a selection of pieces by designers she discovered, many of whom have gone on to establish their names in the international fashion arena. Clothes by Dries van Noten, John Galliano, Jean-Paul Gaultier and Helmut Lang were all bought by Whistles at the start of their careers.

ADDRESS 303 Brompton Road, London SW3 (020 7823 9134)
OPEN Monday to Saturday, 10.00–18.30; Wednesday, 10.00–19.00; Sunday, 12.00–17.00
UNDERGROUND South Kensington

ledbury road

Aimé

One of the newer additions to the design Mecca that is Ledbury Road, Aimé was opened by Val and Vanda Heng Vong, French-born sisters of Cambodian descent, in March 1999. Coming to London to study (Val was doing fashion and Vanda had been studying law), although they immediately loved London life, they missed certain brands and products with which they were familiar in Paris.

Aimé was the answer. Stocking only French designers, it showcases the French fashion, jewellery and homeware. Les Prairies de Paris make very plain but very stylish clothing, Tam Pico designs versatile leather boxes, bins and photoframes, and Petit Bateau is a range of affordable, comfortable basics made from fabrics usually used to manufacture baby-wear.

The store, designed by the sisters, is spread over two levels. One of the walls is lined with photographs and brief biographies of the designers whose products fill the shelves and hang from the rails.

ADDRESS 32 Ledbury Road, London W11 (020 7221 7070)
OPEN Monday to Saturday, 10.30–19.00
UNDERGROUND Notting Hill Gate

Nick Ashley

If the name sounds familiar to you then your hunch is correct – Nick is the youngest son of the late Laura Ashley, whose flowery designs for clothes and homeware opened shops bearing her name all over the world.

Yet flowery designs could not be further from the clothes for which Nick Ashley is making a name. This is a biker shop, albeit a very trendy one. It sells functional clothing designed by Nick himself, as well as bikes and biker gear. This gear ranges from retro goggles, face scarves and gloves to specialised liquid soap for the clothes, and moon-eye stickers for personal decoration on bikes and helmets. The bikes are sold via a noticeboard located by the front door, but passers-by may think that they are lined up outside, as at any one time there are usually at least three bikes leaning against the exterior of the shop.

Ashley was bitten by the biking bug in 1974. After a short spell as an art editor for British *Vogue* magazine, he joined the family business, becoming design director in 1981. His own store was only opened in 1994 and during the interim years he worked on a wide variety of design projects under the Ashley banner.

The versatile clothing that Ashley creates in two annual collections is unique because it is both high-tech and low-key. Modern fabrics such as Microfleece, Ventile Aquatex, Pertex and Polartec and even the divine *faux*-suede Alcantara (even more expensive and more durable than the real thing,) make his clothes particularly appealing to an active but fashion-conscious, crowd of film-, music- and design-industry people. He only produces his designs in black, brown, green and navy (bike clothing is traditionally dark) and this sits well with Londoners who also like to hide beneath layers of dark colours.

Ashley lived above the shop until 1999, holding court with the bikers who visit regularly from Liverpool (he travels north with hardcore riders

to one-stop-shop for store accessories), as well as the local population in search of performance gear that can double as a fashion statement. Last year he moved to Wales, not far from the Ashley family home, and his future plans see him looking east to Japan and a licensing deal with Mitsui, Japan's oldest general trading company. There is no doubt that Nick's bike line will never have the global appeal that his mother's clothes did, but his designs have been spotted astride large pieces of fast-moving machinery further afield than the borders of Notting Hill.

ADDRESS 57 Ledbury Road, London W11 (020 7221 1221)
OPEN Monday to Friday, 10.00–18.00; Saturday, 11.00–18.00; call for opening times in August as they may vary
UNDERGROUND Notting Hill Gate

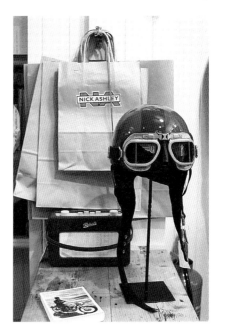

Roger Doyle

Old-school-establishment in terms of reputation, yet forward-looking and inspirational in terms of design, Roger Doyle has the resumé of a jewellery designer whom you could expect to be designing for internationally recognisable jewellery houses like Bulgari or Arpels and Van Cleef and Tiffany.

After an apprenticeship with Cartier in the mid-1960s Doyle worked – by invitation – for Louis Osman on the crown worn by Prince Charles for his investiture as Prince of Wales. He was UK winner of the Diamond International Award, designed a brooch for Margaret Thatcher and has exhibited his work at Harrods , Goldsmith's Hall and at the Victoria & Albert Museum where he has four pieces on permanent display.

In 1996 he opened the shop on Ledbury Road and continues to produce one or two new collections a year. Shapes inspired by shells, branches and twigs in three-colour gold form bracelets and necklaces. Semi-precious stones and black aluminium developed by Doyle are crafted into brooches and rings. He is designing more jewellery for men all the time, but Doyle himself wears only cufflinks.

ADDRESS 38 Ledbury Road, London W11 (020 7727 5797)
OPEN Monday to Friday, 10.00–18.00; Saturday, 11.00–18.00
UNDERGROUND Notting Hill Gate

Simon Finch Rare Books

At first glance Simon Finch Rare Books on Ledbury Road appears more likely to house contemporary design pieces than old books. 'But that was the effect we were after', Finch explains. 'I wanted to showcase books in a modern setting and free them from the dark greens and reds and dusty shelves of the traditional library'. Designer Marina Chan used organic curves to shape the shelving showcase and desk which doubles as a display cabinet. The shop is lit from below by fairy strip lights and colourful fibre optics positioned behind the elongated egg shaped display shelf. The shop always seems open to the public as the frontage is a huge glass plate and the interior predominantly clean white. A striking titanium-clad door and canopy complete the space-age effect.

The Ledbury Road site (opened by Hugh Grant in November 1999) is not his first outlet. Finch had been dealing in antiquarian books from premises at 53 Maddox Street, W1, and a shop in Norfolk. Finch has been collecting books since childhood and dealing in them since his days at university. In his final year he sold more than £90,000 worth of stock and with a 12 per cent commission he was probably better off than your average undergraduate. He is now one of the top ten booksellers in the world and the publicity generated by some of his bigger purchases has undoubtedly enhanced his now international reputation. He paid a world-record auction price for a science manuscript ($2.2 million for the Archimedes palimpsest) and controversially acquired the Turner collection of mathematical books that had been bequeathed to Keele University.

Like an art dealer with a gallery, Finch nurtures his client base. Constantly travelling, searching for rare books and acquiring at auctions, he also provides advice on insurance, restoration and conservation. Every three months he produces a catalogue. One of the most recent was as unusual as the postmodern book that inspired it. B S Johnson's *The Unfor-*

tunates was published in a form that allowed its beginning and end to be read in that order, but readers could mix up the middle of the book as much as they wanted. Finch copied this idea with 'Unchained' and created a delightful limited edition full-colour catalogue featuring many of the books that were available at the new shop when it opened.

The Ledbury Road site houses twentieth-century stock, while Maddox Street continues to house older books and manuscripts. Maddox Street occupies a narrow, hallway-like space connected over six storeys by a spiralling staircase. Chris West designed the shop to make use of limited space and achieved a sense of modernity that is refreshing in the proximity of so many antiquarian books.

Finch is also a partner in the New King's Road Vintage Guitar Emporium (see page 1.4). While bookselling forms his primary business, he has a passion for rock'n'roll that found an outlet through the shop and a recently opened private members club. The Asylum is located just north of Soho (on the corner of Rathbone Place and Percy Street, W1) in a basement space that already had a literary history. Author and collector of Italian futurism Michael Estorick opened The Asylum when Auberon Waugh shut down his literary club, The Academy, and Finch intends to continue to host literary events on site.

ADDRESS 61a Ledbury Road, London W10 (020 7792 3303)
Website www.simonfinch.com
OPEN Monday to Saturday, 10.00–18.00; Sunday 11.00–18.00
UNDERGROUND Notting Hill Gate

ADDRESS 53 Maddox Street, London W1 (020 7499 0974)
OPEN Monday to Friday, 10.00–18.00
UNDERGROUND Oxford Circus

ledbury road

Vent

In Old French 'vent' translates as 'market' or 'sale'. As an architectural term it is a ventilation point. It indicates a specific cut in a coat or jacket. And as an expression it indicates release as in 'vent your emotions'.

Singapore-born Simon Heah opened up this showcase for a little bit of what he fancies at the end 1995. As a reflection of his changing tastes the shop is filled with different things at any given time. There is no time or fashion specification for what you may find. A nineteenth-century hat could fit smartly with a 1970s pant suit. Shoes, fans, gloves, scarves and lights are only some of the items that pass through this tiny shop.

Heah's attitude to the space is more like a storage unit than a commercial shop. He only opens on Fridays and Saturdays and mans the store by himself (this is understandable – the shop becomes full when more than two people occupy it simultaneously). He packs it with odd and fantastic pieces that he has found in markets and auctions across Europe, the USA and Asia and likes to match people to the objects rather than the other way around. His sharp eye has picked out classic Dior coats and rare Ferragamo handbags, but you are as likely to find something he has designed himself. His architectural background has seen him produce lamps and accessories and more recently he been experimenting with a clothing line.

His shop attracts the usual designer-bargain-seeking local folk, but just about everyone related to the design world – be they producer or patron – has passed through it at one time or another. If not physically, as Heah points out, 'at least in spirit'.

ADDRESS 178a Westbourne Grove (entrance in Ledbury Road), London W11 (vent@btinternet. com)
OPEN Friday and Saturday, 11.00 onwards
UNDERGROUND Notting Hill Gate

westbourne grove

Bill Amberg

Leather bag, leather wallet, leather upholstery or even leather floor, Bill Amberg can provide it all. His style philosophy is apparent throughout his designs, which have an elegant simplicity and individual sparkle.

He opened his first (and so far only) shop in trendy Notting Hill less than four years ago. Amberg is currently local to the area and likes the shop's proximity to bus stops and passing trade. But this being the fashionable part of town that it is, that passing trade could easily mean Tim Roth or one of the supermodels or popstars who own his famous fur-lined leather papooses for carrying their equally famous children.

Amberg was born in Northamptonshire, home of the English leather trade. In the 1970s he moved to Australia and furthered his training under antipodean craftsmen, leading to exhibitions in Sydney, Melbourne and Adelaide. On his return to the United Kingdom in 1982 Amberg launched his own leather-design business. By 1984 he was making a name for himself by designing bags for the high-end likes of Liberty and Joseph. Amberg was also responsible for the men's leather line at Paul Smith – brief cases, satchels and, of course, wallets. By 1990, Amberg was ready to begin an export business that focused primarily on the Japanese market. He has since built up the company to incorporate fashion wholesaling, design consultancy, and a special commission service.

These days, retailers of Bill Amberg merchandise include Harrods, Harvey Nichols, The Conran Shop and Selfridges, with exports to the USA and Japan accounting for 60 per cent of business. But apart from overseeing the constantly evolving collection that is available through the stores, most of Amberg's time is filled with the demands of specific commissions and consulting work.

So far the commissions have had him designing and making the lifesaving webbing harness worn by Tom Cruise in *Mission: Impossible*, and

providing leather panelling, doors and display units for Yves Saint Laurent. Amberg is also responsible for the leather reception desk and lift interior at London's style-conscious Metropolitan Hotel and completely leather coating the inside of a ski chalet in Aspen. The list of London restaurants that feature his work is equally impressive: Mirabelle, Quo Vadis, The Square and Dakota.

In fact Amberg's ability to 'do' just about anything in leather recently brought him a slightly more unusual request. A couple who had seen his work in their building asked that he provide them with a leather bed suite. Amberg is particularly proud of this (as yet) one-off and photos of the black leather sheets, pillow slips and bedspread have made it into his personal file.

ADDRESS 10 Chepstow Road, London W2 (020 7727 3560)
OPEN Monday to Saturday, 10.00–18.00; Wednesday, 10.00–19.00
UNDERGROUND Notting Hill Gate

Solange Azagury-Partridge

A woman with a very distinctive name who makes very distinctive jewellery. Solange Azagury-Partridge's shop has been called the most idiosyncratic jewellery shop in London, but sumptuous and divine may be more applicable adjectives.

The shop is actually a giant jewellery box, with ruby and jade velvet-padded walls and a soft leather floor (care of Bill Amberg; see page 5.2). Huge sofas surround the coffee-table-style viewing tables and Azagury-Partridge's work is displayed in small, lit cabinets that appear awkwardly placed on the walls. It is the sort of place where you could spend hours just drinking in the comfort of it all, and Azagury-Partridge is well aware of this as she believes that if people come in to spend a lot of money then they should feel at home while they are debating what to purchase.

Passers-by have no idea of the treasure trove that sits within, as the exterior of the shop is blacked out and a barred grill secures it. The door is also visually blocked, with only a peep hole for staff to identify who has buzzed on the bell. The security is for insurance purposes, as many of the stones that Azagury-Partridge uses are worth small fortunes even before they've been set. But this deceiving facade gave rise to amusing enquiries. When she first opened the shop in 1994, Azagury-Partridge received several phone calls from men trying to make appointments with her staff – they had mistaken the shop's mysterious exterior for that of a discreet brothel.

Azagury-Partridge did not train as a jewellery designer. It was when she became engaged to creative director and screenplay writer Murray Partridge that her life changed course. She did not like the setting on her engagement ring and decided to design one for herself. A friend was so impressed with it that she asked Azagury-Partridge to make another. As did others. Before she knew it, Azagury-Partridge was in the jewellery

Solange Azagury-Partridge

business and seeing clients and designing all day long. This all took place from the couple's apartment. As she had had two children by this time, Azagury-Partridge realised that she must move her work outside in order to create a framework for her professional life.

Both she and her husband were nervous about the financial demands of running a jewellery design business, but they decorated the shop with only £10,000 and the first collection shown there featured fewer than ten pieces. Azagury-Partridge started working with diamonds in 1997, having previously been unable to afford them and only used precious stones when the piece was specially commissioned (and the capital provided) by a client. Her work has been widely admired because it is design- rather than stone-led. She is inspired by architecture rather than nature and this is apparent in many of her rings. The Smartie Ring (featuring enamel shapes coloured to look like chocolate Smarties), the Satyr Ring (red gargoyle-like face) and the Union Jack Ring (British flag set in white gold), are all pieces that have brought her much media attention. You can buy the rings in enamel or precious stone: the difference will change the cost from expensive to very expensive (expect to pay about £10,000 for a diamond ring). She also has a range of watches and has recently started making earrings.

She has high-profile customers, the most famous of whom is Madonna who was photographed for the *Sunday Times Magazine* wearing an Azagury-Partridge necklace and ring.

ADDRESS 171 Westbourne Grove, London W10 (020 7792 0197)
OPEN Monday to Saturday, 11.00–18.00 (visit by appointment)
UNDERGROUND Notting Hill Gate

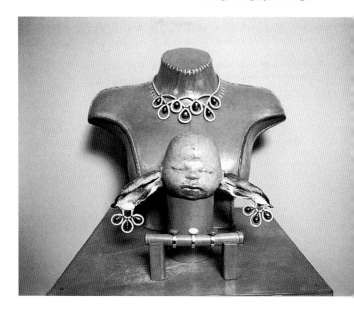

David Champion

David Champion has been designing interiors for many years all over the world in all sorts of houses. The shop, which opened in 1996, was a means of bringing his singular design vision to more people and more homes and is regularly visited by design worshippers and designers alike. Over the past four years it has born a reputation for transformation. Champion and his brother Quentin, who manages the shop with Hubert Zandberg as creative director, are constantly changing the look of the space. Their window is always worth keeping an eye on.

Although Champion discreetly declines to name his clients, the shop is a celebrity drop-in point and many designers visit him for inspiration. The style that he and Zandberg have evolved is very strong and quite masculine, although they are quick to point out that they can go as 'boudoir as you like', if that is the brief. The shop is an eclectic amalgam of decorative objects and antiques – or found objects that may happen to be old. Seagrass mats, Chinese lanterns, ostentatious birdcages and lamps sit happily alongside a collection of organic ornaments such as pods, nautilus shells, ammonites and other fossils. There is a fair amount of abstract African art, and Champion used to sell more Asian art. Yet, unlike many other designers, his interest in art from that part of the world is far more 'Yves Saint Laurent' than 'Zen' (opulent rather than minimal). It is this very distinction that puts Champion in his own league. His vision is strong and unique and derives from a belief that design is an art form rather than a function of practical living.

ADDRESS 199 Westbourne Grove, London W11 (020 7727 6016)
OPEN Monday to Saturday, 10.00–18.00
UNDERGROUND Notting Hill Gate

Christopher Farr

Christopher Farr is an innovator in the unusual design discipline of rugs. Inspired by American painting of the 1950s and '60s – Jackson Pollock, Kenneth Noland, Donald Judd, Robert Motherwell – Farr approaches his rugs in the same way that painters use canvas. Trained in fine art at the Chelsea School of Art and the Slade, Farr's love of colour was broadened to include textiles and dimension when he visited Peru on a scholarship in 1975. He returned to the UK to work with David Black, a pioneering West London rug dealer.

Christopher Farr Handmade Rugs opened in Primrose Hill in 1988. An acclaimed project with the Royal College of Art was the 'Brave New Rugs' show for which Farr selected artists to design rugs. These were handcrafted in one of the world's traditional rug-making centres at Konya in Turkey. It was perhaps the success of a design by Romeo Gigli that inspired Farr to return to the design drawing-board himself.

His first shop closed in February 1999 but the Westbourne Grove premises had already opened in 1996. Designed by James Mair – owner of Viaduct (see page 14.26) – it now sits next to design boutiques that resemble galleries more than shops. And Christopher Farr is no different. His work is beautifully displayed across the walls and floor (fitted by Sharon Bowles of Bowles and Linares interiors). The craftsmanship of the hand-woven rugs is apparent under examination, but the blocks of colour rather than miniature motifs mean that they still fulfil their practical function. Whether hung on the wall or partially hidden underneath furniture the work of Christopher Farr and those he commissions is incredibly impressive.

ADDRESS 212 Westbourne Grove, London W10 (020 7792 5761)
OPEN Monday to Saturday, 11.00–18.00
UNDERGROUND Notting Hill Gate

Glazed and Amused

A witty name for a witty shop. Glazed and Amused is one of several paint-your-own-design-on-crockery shops to hit London, a recent import from the USA. Initially popular with children, Glazed and Amused broke the mould by staying open late and allowing adults to bring their own snacks and beverages (including alcohol) with them.

After you have chosen your ceramic 'canvas' (napkin rings, plates, bowls, cups and saucers are the standard fare), you sit down, pour yourself a beverage and get creative with your glazes. The staff are on hand to give advice and will take your masterpiece when you've finished and fire it in the kiln.

Whether the final result is mediocre or masterpiece, founders Bettina Panahizadi and Ted Wilson say the emphasis is more on fun than fashion. With plans to open up even more branches (another outlet opened in SW18 this year), their formula is proving popular. Unlike its glazes, Glazed and Confused looks set to run and run.

ADDRESS 3 Chepstow Road, London W11 (020 7792 9394)
OPEN Tuesday to Wednesday, Friday, Sunday, 11.00–18.00; Thursday, 11.00–21.00; Saturday, 10.00–18.00
UNDERGROUND Notting Hill Gate

ADDRESS 424 Garratt Lane, London SW18 (020 8944 8060)
OPEN Tuesday, Thursday to Sunday, 11.00–18.00; Wednesday, 11.00–21.00
RAIL Earlsfield

Dinny Hall

After graduating in 1983 from Central St Martin's, the art school that lists Alexander McQueen, John Galliano, Stella McCartney and Antoni and Alison among its alumni, Dinny Hall set up a studio in Soho and began to make jewellery. Within a year she had been asked to design a collection for Rifat Ozbek, whose Middle Eastern influences were complemented by Hall's simple styles. This attention brought her more commissions and she has since worked with Bruce Oldfield, Ben di Lisi and Isaac Mizrahi.

Hall stood out in the 1980s when most popular jewellery was opulent, large and brash. Single pearls on long gold chains, petite drop earrings and miniature amethyst crosses made her sought after by the likes of Madonna, Dawn French, Ralph Fiennes and Ralph Lauren as well as the general public. In 1986 she wrote a book, *Creative Jewellery,* and three years later was awarded the title of Accessory Designer of the Year by the British Fashion Council. In 1992 Hall opened her first – and flagship – store, designed by Munkenbeck and Marshall and fitting in nicely with her design-conscious neighbours on Westbourne Grove. The huge plate-glass window and panelled wood door do not look like those of a typically intimidating jewellery store. Instead, Dinny Hall is breezy, bright and welcoming.

The rise and rise of Hall continued and in 1995 she opened a second store at 54 Fulham Road. In 1996 she was voted Jewellery Designer of the Year by the readers of *Marie Claire.* She has several diffusion ranges, which can be tracked down in chain stores throughout the UK.

ADDRESS 200 Westbourne Grove, London W10 (020 7792 3913)
OPEN Monday to Friday, 11.00–19.00; Saturday, 10.00–18.00
UNDERGROUND Notting Hill Gate

Dinny Hall

Mission

Mission is a concept that blurs the parameters between shop and gallery. It has pioneered the technique of hosting themed exhibitions and selling work through these shows. Mission has shown furniture next to fashion accessories next to lampshades next to books. Old, new, in-house design or internationally recognisable label, you never know what you will find on display, or how long it is going to be there.

Mission was opened in May 1998 by Serb-Cypriot Misha Stefan and his girlfriend Yvonne Courtney. The name was her idea and reflects their partnership, being a punning combination of parts of their names. Stefan had studied at the Architectural Association School but has become a designer rather than an architect. Courtney is a public-relations consultant under the banner of Courtney Communications. The space on Hereford Road was designed by Stefan and displays his distinctive curved space-age yet retro style. Pastel walls, organic curves, split levels and diffused lighting give Mission a feel of modern tranquility.

Mission takes an active role in encouraging the work of certain designers. Promoting Barnaby Tuke, who is now famous for his carved concrete stools and upholstered recliners (one of which stared out from every magazine rack in the country on the cover of *Elle Deco* in 1999), and Patrick Frederickson, who makes warm luna lights and coat racks that double as wall decorations, has given Mission a reputation that is allowing them to compete on an international level.

One of the first shows to exemplify this was the Diesel 'Retrospective/ Futurspective' exhibition in 1998. The Italian jeans label showed their classic and contemporary designs and fashion junkies flocked to the space. This has since been followed by other topical exhibitions that included a white exhibition ('Carte Blanche') and a spectacular show ('The Earth is (Not) Flat') hosted by Knoll and featuring the work of Maya

Lin. Some of the shows give Stefan the opportunity to showcase his own sought-after pieces. He is part of Tonic, the design collective that also includes input from Michael Wolfson and Patrick Frederickson. Their Yo-Yo range has been particularly successful for its huge comfy chairs and versatile modernist-influenced shelving units and coffee tables.

While the shop-cum-gallery is no longer unique in London, Mission remains a pioneer in the promotion of young international talent.

ADDRESS 45 Hereford Road, London w2 (020 7792 4633)
OPEN Monday to Friday, 11.00–18.00; Saturday by appointment
UNDERGROUND Bayswater

Ogier

Frenchman Yves Ogier lived in Asia before coming to London with his wife Niki Frei in 1999. He immediately set up along the stretch of design shops on Westbourne Grove and started selling furniture and utensils from Singapore and the Far East as well as lighting from France.

Lighting was obviously a personal passion as Ogier designed and sold some of his own hanging glass-beaded variety. But it was the cactus-style green and white lights of design team 212 (Mahmoud Akram and Thierry Legrand) that caught the public's attention and their simple, striking design that epitomised what Ogier and Frei were hoping to achieve with their shop. Fabric-shade lamps by Sharon Marston and copper and bronze shade hanging lamps complete Ogier's eye-catching range.

Living in Asia had introduced the couple to simple designs – chopsticks, bowls, bed linen and napkins – that they believed could enhance the look of modern European furniture. The space itself is somewhat masculine and cold, but Ogier's smattering of colour, on cushions and from the lights, makes a stark skeleton appear warm and welcoming. As they grow – in stock and reputation – Ogier and Frei will use the two-storey space to showcase some of the designers that they are introducing to London.

ADDRESS 177 Westbourne Grove, London W11 (020 7229 0783)
OPEN Monday to Saturday, 10.00–18.00
UNDERGROUND Notting Hill Gate

Planet Organic

The model of a modern healthy-food outlet, Planet Organic was opened in 1995 by Renee Elliot and Jonathan Dwek. Both had come up with the idea of a natural-food supermarket, rather than the usual small health-food shop, and when they met (ironically at Wild Oats, the UK branch of a US chain of healthfood shops), they were able to turn their dream into reality.

With a mission to provide healthy alternatives for diet and body-care, Planet Organic stocks rice noodles for those who don't want to eat wheat, organic cheeses and wines, fluoride-free toothpaste, vegan pesto for lactose-intolerant vegetarians, potato flour and even eco-friendly toilet paper. Every day deliveries of fresh bio-dynamic (one step up from organic; where produce is planted and reaped within certain astrological parameters on farms that are completely self-sufficient) produce, including a wide range of fruits and vegetables, arrive and are displayed in a colourful array near the front of the store. The meat counter also adheres to strict organic guidelines and is manned by six fully qualified butchers who are trained to deal with the most unusual of dietary requests.

Apart from some very unusual foodstuffs, Planet Organic also stocks a vast range of vitamin and mineral supplements and is expanding its range of natural body-care products. The organic make-up range from Dr Hauschka is particularly popular – perhaps most notably with Jerry Hall. And she is not the only celebrity regular. Tom Cruise, Lulu, Sean Connery and Jade Jagger have all pushed trolleys around Planet's aisles.

Elliot and Dwek split company somewhat acrimoniously in 1999 but Elliot is now expanding the business and there are plans to open other branches around the capital. Apart from the supermarket fundamentals, Planet has a fresh juice bar and bookstore where customers can read up

on health and diet. The supermarket also provides a delivery service and mail order for vitamins and supplements.

The success of Planet Organic has inspired larger supermarkets to start stocking health-conscious products. Elliot was happy that 1999 was the year that organic went mainstream. She will be even happier when this decade sees Planet Organic itself go mainstream.

ADDRESS 42 Westbourne Grove, London W2 (020 7221 7171)
OPEN Monday to Saturday, 9.00–20.00; Sunday, 11.00–17.00
UNDERGROUND Bayswater

Space

This is definitely a shop for those fortunate enough to have some in their homes. Space was bought from Tom Dixon, now head of design at Habitat, by its current owner – Emma Oldham – in 1995. At that time it was situated on the All Saint's Road, but in 1996 moved to its current – appropriately chic – Westbourne Grove premises.

Space is one of a group of shops on Westbourne Grove which are so stylish that they are almost intimidating to enter. This should not deter potential purchasers or mere eye-candy seekers, as the attitude once you enter Space is friendly and helpful. Oldham is obviously proud of her shop and the work of the designers that she showcases through it, and is always happy to talk to interested customers about their history and work.

Oldham herself has a design background and was making scarves and freelancing as an interiors stylist before she settled into her own space. Although she does continue to have some creative outlets through a line of opulent bed linen as well as bean bags and cushions, the defining factor of Space is its status as a retail gallery; literally providing the space for young designers to exhibit their work.

Monica Lipkin's orange glowing floor lights and Jeremy Lord's colour-changing light box are among the pieces that Oldham has displayed. She holds irregular openings and focuses on displaying one designer at a time. One of her most successful 'shows' featured work by wicker-light-designer Michael Sodeau. Abigail Simpson and Sophie Cook both produce ceramics that Oldham sells; Owen George's sexy cube seats and Tom Kirk's lights are available here.

Oldham finds artists and designers by travelling to trade shows (although she claims that they serve the sole purpose of displaying every-thing that she should avoid) and looking at work that people bring to her. Having always wanted Space to be an evolving business, she recently

Space

set up Space PR, which looks after the press around the artists that she deals with. Her sister Charlie Coe also joined her as a partner.

Like most of the design-conscious shops on this stretch of Westbourne Grove, Space receives its quota of famous visitors. Bjork, Damon Albarn, Robbie Williams and Joe Fiennes have all shopped here, as has Peter Mandelson, purchaser of a Balzac chair.

ADDRESS 214 Westbourne Grove, London W11 (020 729 6533)
WEBSITE www.spaceshop.co.uk
OPEN Monday to Saturday, 10.00–18.00
UNDERGROUND Notting Hill Gate

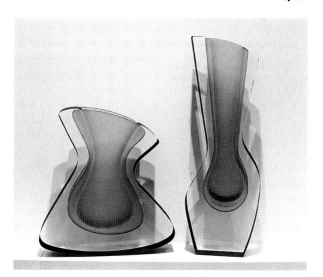

Themes and Variations

'Themes and Variations' is the title of a series of 365 plates by Italian designer Piero Fornasetti. French-born Lilianne Fawcett took the name and opened her shop with an exhibition of the plates. The year was 1984 and she had been selling post-war design objects on Portobello Road with the help of her friend Julianna Medda.

Fawcett is a woman with vision. When Themes and Variations opened, visitors to the shop would snicker at some of the pieces she sold. At that time post-war design had not become collectable and sought-after. Nowadays, museum curators and the design-conscious Westbourne Grove crowd make up her most regular customers.

She acquires her stock of 1950s furniture and 1960s–1970s Scandinavian jewellery in both Europe and the USA. What was originally a very time-consuming search has eased off as the reputation of the shop has become more widespread and people holding relevant items are as likely to seek out Fawcett as she is them.

Designs by Carlo Mollino, Gio Ponti and Arne Jacobson have all passed through her hands. Fawcett is very fond of 1950s glass and 1960s jewellery. Original 1960s rings by Mary Quant and Fornasetti ties are also staples of this very fine design store.

ADDRESS 231 Westbourne Grove, London W11 (020 7727 5531)
OPEN Monday to Friday, 10.00–13.00, 14.00–18.00; Saturday, 10.00–18.00
UNDERGROUND Notting Hill Gate

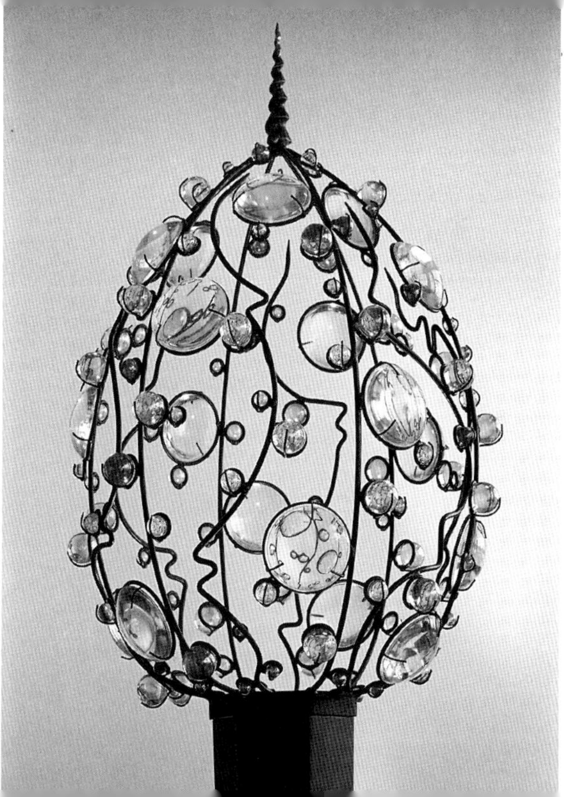

Vessel

Named for that which you'll find within, Vessel is a self-proclaimed one-stop shop for all manner of table- and glassware. Yet that definition does not do the shop-cum-gallery justice as each of the pieces on display seem as though they would sit as easily in the hallowed cases of a design museum as they would on your dining table.

It was on a vacation in Switzerland that Nadia Demetriou Ladas first fell in love with the colourful 1950s glassware that would finally lead to her opening Vessel with her designer (and life) partner Angel Monzon. What began as a hobby, amassing her favourite pieces, grew into a collection that she could no longer contain at home. Ladas was also aware that there was no outlet in London that simply addressed today's eating habits. Where once people might use three glasses, two knives and several spoons during a properly served dinner, now a main course could just as acceptably be eaten from a bowl with chopsticks with a sushi-rolling mat doubling as a place mat.

Vessel sells the work of young British ceramist Bodo Sperlein, whose organic bowls double as vases and candle dishes. They are also the main UK retailer of Italian art-glass company Arcade whose designer-director Ivan Baj's work is housed in several museums. One of Vessel's more fun lines comes from Swedish glass manufacturer Pukeburg. Its range of sand-blasted drinking glasses and decanters is functional as well as aesthetic and includes six cone-shaped shot glasses. Ensconced in wooden casing and with rounded bases that mean they cannot freestand, they defy sipping and demand shot drinking.

Monzon designed Vessel on two floors so that upstairs could be dedicated to retail and the basement reserved for curated exhibitions. In the short time since it opened, Vessel has already showcased work by New York-based jewellery designer Ted Muehling who developed porcelain

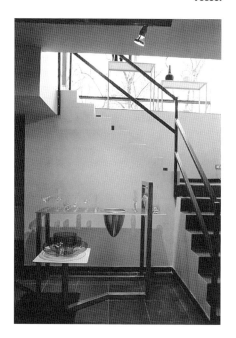

pieces for both the body and the home in an exhibition called 'Alchemy and Art'. Isabel Hamm is another of their protegées and – unlike Muehling – is one of the younger designers for whom they also act as agent. Her glasswork comes in bright acid colours and her bowls are designed to rock gently under pressure.

Although it is fairly new, Vessel's reputation is spreading fast and wide. The exhibition schedule for 2000 has featured an exciting window display by Simon Doone, the Barney's art director responsible for the highly successful book (movie rights in which have apparently been bought by Madonna), *Confessions of a Window Dresser*.

ADDRESS 114 Kensington Park Road, London W11 (020 7727 8001)
OPEN Monday to Saturday, 10.30–18.30; Sunday, 11.00–17.00
UNDERGROUND Notting Hill Gate

westbourne grove

Wild At Heart

A well-groomed flower shop for the well-groomed folk who patrol Westbourne Grove and Ledbury Road in search of beautiful things with which to enhance their lives. And Wild at Heart can certainly provide beautiful bouquets, and corsages, cake flowers, button flowers, bridesmaids' posies and any number of vase, urn, pew and pedestal arrangements.

Nikki Tibble's brainchild is spread over two venues, only a couple of hundred metres apart. Both share the fact that they are very distinctive in design. The first to open was on Turquoise Island, the azure-coloured lavatory designed by Piers Gough. Needing more space, Tibble commissioned Future Systems to design the shop in Ledbury Road. Their design was derived from the idea that flowers are organic structures; they are not about straight lines and they evolve as they grow. Future Systems' use of this premise resulted in a stark white two-floor space with water vases built into the curved couch that encircles the ground level.

In the basement Tibble and her staff make up the daily orders before delivering them to top London hotels. Wild at Heart has also supplied flowers to The Ritz, The Victoria & Albert Museum and Westminster Abbey and has worked for Chanel, Ralph Lauren, Gucci and Vogue.

Wild at Heart's reputation for style now goes before it and Tibble soon plans to open up a flower school. Ikebana eat your heart out!

ADDRESS 49a Ledbury Road and Turquoise Island, 222 Westbourne Grove, London W11 (020 7727 3095)
OPEN Monday to Saturday, 8.00–19.00
UNDERGROUND Notting Hill Gate

notting hill/
holland park

The Cross

Pretty in pink, lovely in lilac, rosy in red or blooming in baby-blue: The Cross will tickle any girl's fancy. This little success story of a store is as sweet as the shop itself. Best friends forever, Sam Robinson and Sarah Keane dreamed of opening a boutique selling all the girlie-type things that they themselves love to wear, sit on, wrap themselves in, give, smell of, and bathe in. They discovered that they have popular taste and have put a quiet Holland Park backstreet on every girl in London's shopping map.

The two-floor treasure chest is full to bursting with flower-covered shower caps, chenille and velvet scarves, furry throws and organza appliquéd bags. The wood floors are painted in white to match the walls and give a clean, homey feel to the whole shop. As well as accessories, The Cross is known for supplying Dosa's tumbled-silk slip dresses, Palmiero's clam-diggers and shoes by Sigerson Morrison.

ADDRESS 141 Portland Road, London W11 (020 7727 6760)
OPEN Monday to Saturday, 10.30–18.00
UNDERGROUND Holland Park

Graham and Green

Spread out over three separate premises on a block shared by a health-conscious juice bar and a *feng-shui*-conscious paint shop, Graham and Green provides just about everything necessary for an enhanced lifestyle. From soft suede cushions to plastic wash-bags covered in swimming gold-fish, these shops are choc-a-bloc with items you never knew you needed. But a stroll through them will have most customers wondering how they lived without pastel cashmere pashminas, bamboo table mats and turned-wood chesspiece salt and pepper pots.

It was on Easter Monday in 1974 that Antonia Graham opened the doors of the first Graham and Green at 7 Elgin Crescent. Apart from the three on the Crescent, she has since opened another outlet in Chalk Farm and plans more in the near future. Back in 1974 she was a young mother with a baby son. More than 25 years later, that same son, Jamie, has taken on the role of design director.

The two share a love of travel to remote places and have used trips to Turkey, Laos, India and Afghanistan to collect kelims, silk robes, coloured-glass mosque chandeliers, saris and other artefacts that fill the shops, making them regular haunts for those in search of ethnic-knacks.

ADDRESS 4, 7 and 10 Elgin Crescent, London W11 (020 7727 4594)
OPEN Monday to Saturday, 10.00–18.00; Sunday, 12.00–17.00
UNDERGROUND Notting Hill Gate

Mattamondo

'Crazy world' is the meaning of this crazy-sounding Italian word. Yet it becomes appropriate when it is put in the context of Italian Christina Graham's African-artefact-stocked shop. Graham arrived in London ten years ago where she began working for charities that included Save the Rhino and The Wilderness Trust. These jobs led her to Africa and travels on that continent exposed her to a wealth of handcrafted furniture, utensils and art.

Having worked in charities, Graham came to believe that donating money is not always the best way to help people in poverty-stricken environments. Instead, if they are given the means to produce goods that can be traded, they have an incentive to learn a skill and use this skill to enhance their position in life. Graham arrived at the conclusion that a retail space would provide that outlet for community based groups and Mattamondo was born.

Due to its handcrafted nature, stock in the shop changes and cannot always be replaced – if you like something here you'd better buy it immediately. The brightly patterned bowls made from packaging, commissioned from an AIDS project in South Africa, have proven especially popular. South Africa provides Mattamondo with beautiful cutlery (cast in brass and silver plate in the shape of fish) and cast-iron cooking pots as well. These pots – heavy and black – are typical of those used by many African families, but Graham has seen them leave her shop to become plant pots and BBQ accessories.

Graham has also collected sculpted soaps from Vermont and pieces from the local London area such as leatherbound notebooks by Barbara Wiggins. But her awareness of the need to support under-privileged groups in Africa and the fact that she is taking a degree in Zulu studies means that the shop is definitely Afrocentric in terms of stock. Ceramic

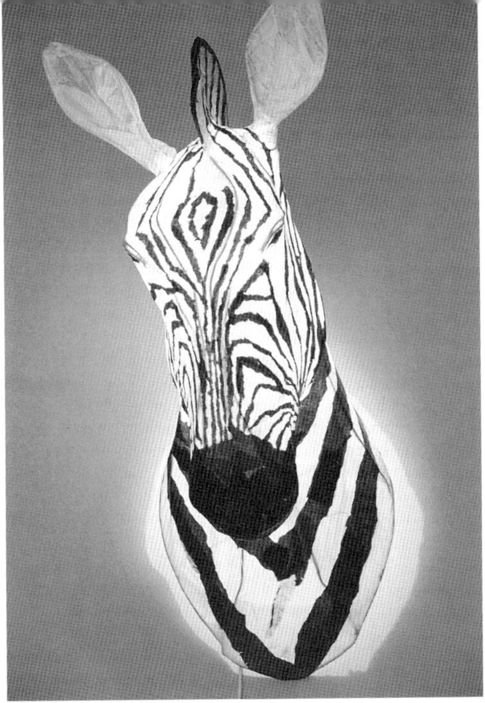

bead necklaces made by single mothers in Nairobi and wicker furniture made by a tribe in Zimbabwe where unemployment has reached around 60 per cent of the population give every piece in Mattamondo a story. Graham herself remembers the time she was looking to buy some baskets made from telephone wire. She spent hours walking to a tiny village but within minutes was surrounded by local women, eager to sell the pieces and have a little money of their own. Mattamondo is not a charity shop, but in the style of charity shops it knows that craftwork brings communities together and that by supporting them traditions and communities may survive.

ADDRESS 22 Powis Terrace, London W11 (020 7229 5669)
OPEN Tuesday to Saturday, 11.00–18.00
UNDERGROUND Westbourne Park

Ovo

Ovo – the base of words referring to eggy things, such as ovoid and ovum – is the hatchling of Linda Sparks and Eran Palatnik. They opened the shop as a showcase for Sparks' interior design and lifestyle ideas in early 1999 and have watched the top end of Portobello Road slowly attract more like-minded retailers.

Sparks was originally a hairdresser on the King's Road but began working in interior design and moved to New York to pursue this passion at Parson's Design School. She returned to the UK two years ago, but Palatnik, whose primary career is in film, remains based in the USA.

The American influence is apparent in their stock. Jonathan Adler, a New York-based potter, produces neutrally glazed, solid plates and bowls that sit comfortably next to Fire Form's Californian glassware and Galerkin sofas and chairs. The chunky furniture has a 1950s feel and is also imported from California.

As Sparks's time is now spent mainly in the UK, she is trying to source more European design and among the noteworthy results are the versatile fairy lights from Dutch designers 100 ASA. Made from discarded transparent film cases, the lights are both decorative and effective, as are the Droog lights that Sparks also stocks in the 'comfortable Zen' environment she endeavours to maintain.

ADDRESS 339 Portobello Road, London W10 (020 8960 7296)
OPEN Monday to Saturday, 11.00–18.00
UNDERGROUND Ladbroke Grove

Screen Face

Screen Face is a make-up shop all about imagination. This is primarily due to the fact that it started life as a shop for make-up artists. Magdelene Gaffney launched her business in 1985, with the help of her husband John Danvers. She had begun working as a make-up artist for the BBC in 1963 (five years before colour television came to Britain), and moved into film work more than 20 years ago.

Gaffney's wealth of experience meant that she knew exactly what equipment the market was missing. She and Danvers originally sold durable, versatile make-up boxes and mirrors that would not break as they were dragged on and off planes and around the world on shoots. The reputation of these boxes and mirrors for durability remains one of Screen Face's biggest selling points.

The past 15 years have seen Screen Face expand rapidly. Gaffney bought an Italian make-up line and created a range of make-up under the Screen Face name. She and Danvers built the company into a 'one-stop-shop'; an emporium where make-up artists would be able to buy everything that they needed, no matter how obscure or strange.

And some of the products that they stock will seem strange to those who are not in the business. Screen Face is internationally famous for the fake blood that it manufactures in-house. Screen Face blood was used in *Braveheart*, and theirs was the blood that Steven Spielberg insisted be used all the way through *Saving Private Ryan* – obviously a massive order.

Big Hollywood names are nothing new to Gaffney. She was chief make-up artist on Jane Campion's *Portrait of a Lady* (powdering the noses of Nicole Kidman, John Malkovich, Shelley Winters, Barbara Hershey and Martin Donovan) and has worked on *The Mission, Raiders of the Lost Ark, Rosencrantz and Guildenstern are Dead, Sleeping With the Fishes, Black Beauty, A Dry White Season, War and Remembrance,* and *Return*

Return to Oz, among many other films. This phenomenal career has been recognised by four Emmy nominations, but has not affected Gaffney in any obvious way. She remains true to her Irish roots and is delightfully down to earth.

Screen Face supplies make up for many major movies. It runs much of its business through a mail-order catalogue and their astoundingly professional website. It has a rapid and efficient delivery service. From travel bags and brushes to heated eye-lash curlers and fold-out boxes, Screen Face provides value for money – obviously the reason that models such as Linda Evangelista and Jerry Hall have long been regular customers.

The Powis Terrace shop was expanded to include a make-up testing salon. In June 1997 Screen Face opened a second shop in Monmouth Street, WC2. This more central location is used by ordinary rather than industry customers, but is stocked with all the Screen Face goodies. There are more than 80 skin tones in its foundation range, the largest selection of eyelashes in London, and a multitude of colours in its crêpe-hair range. Screen Face is the European distributor of an original 1960s make-up line by Vincent Kehoe.

Screen Face is a success story that will continue with every new film it supplies and every girl who walks out of one of the shops carrying her first pot of party glitter.

ADDRESS 24 Powis Terrace, London W11 (020 7221 8289)
WEBSITE www.screenface.co.uk
OPEN Monday to Saturday, 9.00–18.00
UNDERGROUND Westbourne Park

Paul Smith

The United Kingdom's most successful fashion designer (with an annual worldwide turnover of £173 million), Paul Smith set up his label more than 30 years ago. Although he has opened up more than ten shops in Britain and has more than 200 in Japan and Asia, Westbourne House, as it is called, is very different from his other outlets.

Smith had long dreamt of having a shop in a house. In 1996 Westbourne House became available and Smith, under the supervision of architect Sophie Hicks, converted the entire former Victorian family residence into a shop. The house is approached through a small garden and the six rooms are arranged on three floors (the basement is used by the staff only), each leading off on opposite sides of the glass and acrylic central staircase. This staircase is the focal point upon entry and is the main indicator that, while the exterior of the building has merely been restored to its former Victorian glory, the interior has been gutted and completely modernised.

Each room has been given a name and a theme. The Kensington Room on the ground floor is the main womenswear department and was designed to resemble a private dressing room that might belong to the lady of the house. With grey taffeta curtains, a glass-bubble Tom Dixon lamp, white snakeskin-covered chairs and a mirrored table, the room – like the house – combines the modern and the traditional. Smith's extensive accessories range is available in the Dining Room. In the middle of this room is a huge dining-style table which is actually a display cabinet filled with watches, pens, leather goods (such as wallets) and glasses. Bags and hats are pinned to the walls, replacing pictures, and limited-edition books and photographs cover the remaining wall and surface space.

Upstairs on the landing is a wall full of pictures that are all personal to Smith. The Archer Room – home to informal clothing for men – is

Paul Smith

located on the first floor. Opposite this is the most fun room in West-bourne House – the Play Room. Full of squeaking toys, mini bean-bags, toy cameras and even child-sized scooters, the Play Room is home to Smith's childrenswear collection. It is colourful and vibrant and the Tom Dixon-designed igloo changing-room and funky jiggling installations in the floor all contribute to an appropriately innovative environment.

Up the final flight of stairs are the Randell and Gurston Rooms. Smith's recent shoe collection is available in the Randell Room, as are his classic suits for men. In the Gurston Room Savile Row-trained tailors measure up customers for Smith's bespoke suits. Jars of buttons, bales of fabric and cardboard patterns attest to the superior workmanship that takes place here.

ADDRESS 122 Kensington Park Road, London W11 (020 7727 3553)
OPEN Monday to Thursday, 10.30–18.30; Friday, Saturday, 10.00–18.30
UNDERGROUND Notting Hill Gate

Squirreled away at the very top of Portobello Road, 367 has been the home of Shirley Day since September 1999. It was opened as 'Shirley Day at 367' and sold furniture, *objets d'art*, clothing and hats, but in summer 2000 Day's space was taken over by design duo Olowu Golding.

Shirley Day met Duro Olowu and Elaine Golding at an exhibition at Mission (see page 5.22), when the clothing and shoe designers were working from a small outlet on nearby Artisian Road. They were looking for more space and Day was looking for less as she wished to spend more time pursuing her career as an artist and sculptor. The three agreed that Olowu Golding would take on the site as a work and retail space for their fashion and shoe production, while Day would keep her furniture finds passing through the premises as well.

Day's vision meets that of Olowu Golding at a very high-end level. She kept the space packed with rare pieces of twentieth-century French furniture. She has shown 1930s chairs from the Blue Bar in Cannes that may well have supported the bottoms of Orson Welles and Brigitte Bardot, and hats by Pip Hackett. Crockery, bags, cushions, wardrobes, lamps and textiles all reflect Day's international experience in interior consulting.

Olowu, with his Jamaican/Nigerian heritage, shares Day's international perspective and his handmade clothes, along with Golding's handmade shoes are sought after by a crowd at ease inside Gucci, Prada and Versace. Olowu and Golding intend to continue to use 367 as an outlet for ideas, and a space from which to launch their couture philosophy on a larger scale.

ADDRESS 367 Portobello Road, London W10 (020 8964 9457)
OPEN Tuesday to Saturday, 11.00–18.00, or by appointment
UNDERGROUND Ladbroke Grove

victoria/pimlico

Erickson Beamon

Erikson Beamon is responsible for the ultimate costume jewellery. What began in New York in 1983 as a partnership between Karen Erickson and Vicky Sarge has grown into an internationally recognised jewellery label with a client list that reads like a who's who of the high-fashion, music and film worlds.

Erickson Beamon designs all the jewellery to accompany the runway collections of Givenchy, Armani, McQueen, Galliano, Dries van Noten, DKNY, Christian Dior, Rifat Ozbek, Molinari and Ghost. Its work is sought after and owned by Nicole Kidman, Cher, Whitney Houston, Jerry Hall, Madonna, Sharon Stone, Bjork and Joan Collins (one of their favourite customers).

The London store, opened in 1994, is its only retail outlet. Sarge had moved to London in 1985 to expand the business and married and settled here soon after. She still designs much of the jewellery but is assisted by a team of younger designers, some of whom have gone on to establish names for themselves. Metal-worker Lesley Vik-Waddel and Sarah Harmony, who designs many of the pieces for Alexander McQueen, are both represented by Erickson Beamon.

The work here is versatile and inventive. Strands of pearls strung to hang delicately on the breastbone as well as around the neck, chokers held up with twelve or more rows of crystal beading, headpieces and body-adornments mark out Erickson Beamon as among the most striking and innovative costume-jewellery designers in the world.

ADDRESS 38 Elizabeth Street, London SW1 (020 7259 0202)
OPEN Monday to Friday, 10.00–18.00; Saturday, 11.00–17.00
UNDERGROUND Victoria

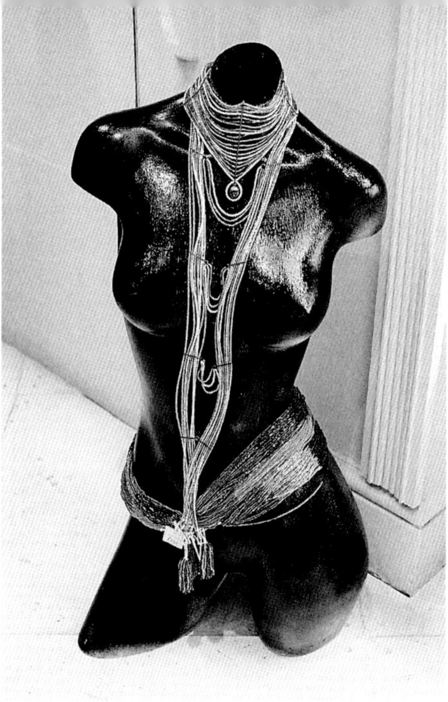

victoria/pimlico

Selina Blow

Selina Blow has a lot of character. The tailored suits that cut her name in the world of fashion design are an eclectic mix of inspired brilliance and English eccentricity; a reflection of her own influences. She comes from an eclectic family with artistic and political connections. Her great-grandfather was instrumental in gaining independence for Sri Lanka, while her great-grandmother worked on women's voting rights there. Her grandfather – Detmar Blow – was a celebrated art-and-crafts architect.

Selina Blow – herself half Sri Lankan – began designing smartly tailored suits with Nehru coats using eye-catching fabrics sourced from all over the world and sold wholesale. Her trademark shop opened in 1995. This space on Elizabeth Street was originally shared with Lulu Guinness, but their separate successes saw Guinness open two shops of her own while Blow took over the whole of the original premises. Blow still stocks Guinness's handbags alongside others by The Jacksons, as well as hats and shoes and other pieces by Georgina von Etzdorf.

Alhtough modern, Blow's suits have a timeless quality, also expressed in the decor of the store. Comfortable sheepskin-covered beanbags and cushions sit on the seagrass matting of the floor; scented candles by Artisan are displayed in elegant cabinets and Blow's classic tailoring hangs from suspended rails throughout the split-room shop. The most recent addition to her suits and separates – which include satin and velvet dresses as well as a cashmere line – is a menswear range.

ADDRESS 42 Elizabeth Street, London SW1 (020 7730 2449)
OPEN Monday to Saturday, 10.00–18.00; Saturday, 11.00–17.00
UNDERGROUND Victoria

Philip Treacy

Ask anyone for the name of a milliner and if they can think of just one, it is highly likely that the name will be Philip Treacy. Even before he graduated from the Royal College of Art in 1990 Treacy had worked with John Galliano, Rifat Ozbek and Victor Edelstein. Within the next five years he had opened his own showroom, from where he still works and sells on Elizabeth Street, begun long-standing relationships with both Chanel and Karl Lagerfeld, created three shows and a ready-to-wear line and been awarded British Accessory Designer of the Year three times. Treacy was to win that honour twice more, in 1996 and 1997.

The originality and brilliance of his hats defy description. Treacy has virtually single-handedly put millinery on the fashion map. His hats make statements, both in style and shape. His recent Millennium collection caused a furore both in New York and London when he had Grace Jones growling down the catwalk in his 'Merlin the Magician' silver metal cone hat stretching her already impressive profile to an even greater height.

Treacy is not frightened of his hats overwhelming a woman or her outfits: his headpieces (or sometimes, eyebrow- or even face-pieces), actually *make* a woman or her outfit. He uses many of the traditional milliner's materials – such as straw, felt and feathers – but he will position the feathers to fall over the face, appearing to cascade like teardrops. the straw will be so deconstructed that the hat becomes a series of fine bands rather than a solid structure. Or felt will be pushed into a shape so exaggerated that it stylishly parodies more conservative versions.

The fantastic creations that he had wrought over the past few years have placed his work in several museum and gallery shows (including 'Cutting Edge' at the Victoria & Albert Museum, and 'One Hundred Years of Art and Fashion' at the Hayward Gallery).

Philip Treacy

A growing empire all stems from Treacy's tiny showroom near Victoria Station. Visitors may enter at their own peril because his rotund little dog, aptly named Miss Pig (or Lord Pig, depending on Treacy's mood), is often there checking out customers at ankle level. Treacy, however, will be dealing with you only from the neck up. Mad as a hatter? Treacy most definitely is.

ADDRESS 69 Elizabeth Street, London SW1 (020 7259 9605)
OPEN Monday to Friday, 10.00–18.00
UNDERGROUND Victoria

soho

Agent Provocateur

The English have been associated with prudery and modesty for too long. Or so thought Joseph Corré and Serena Rees when they opened this naughty little den of inequity in a sordid Soho backstreet. Once the porn centre of London, Soho is still home to several strip lounges and adult-video stores, but the fashionable restaurants and bars that have moved into the area over the past decade have virtually eradicated its seedy reputation. Nevertheless, the opening of Agent Provocateur in the area was amusingly appropriate and caused minor scandal, at least with the violin makers who work out of the building opposite. They found the sight of 'Diane', the voluptuous mannequin with her luscious upturned bottom, and the Christmas window festivities which featured an erect-penis-shaped tree spurting cotton snow, too much to bear and replaced their clear window with frosted glass.

Joe Corré is the son of the once-controversial couple Vivienne Westwood and Malcolm McLaren. His mother designed the foxy outfits worn by the floor-staff. The shop is styled to resemble a boudoir, with frilly brassieres and matching knickers spilling out from dark wooden drawers and glass cabinets.

Corré and Rees aimed to create a range of lingerie that would titillate and amuse both wearers and their partners. The formula has proved very successful – in 1997 a second boutique opened in Knightsbridge's Pont Street and recently a third shop (that doubles as the Edra Mazzei – designer of bright, loud furniture – Showroom), opened at 119 Charterhouse Street, EC1. Seamed stockings, suspenders and garter belts are reminiscent of an underwear era long gone, yet this is what Agent Provocateur is about. By matching bras with pants with belts with shoes with jewellery they have evolved a sexy line that is fun and individual.

Since the opening of the Broadwick Street branch in 1994, Agent

Agent Provocateur

Provocateur has remained in the public eye through a series of events. In September 1995 it hosted the final of the Agent Provocateur girl competition; it is responsible for the sexy uniforms worn by the staff at Café de Paris, and has launched a line of bikinis. In 1997 Agent Provocateur lingerie was featured as part of the Victoria & Albert Museum's 'Cutting Edge' exhibition. And even more recently they have broken into the mainstream, taking on responsibility for part of one of the world's most respectable lingerie lines, that of Marks & Spencer.

ADDRESS 6 Broadwick Street, London W1 (020 7439 0229)
WEBSITE www.agentprovocateur.com
OPEN Monday to Saturday, 11.00–19.00
UNDERGROUND Tottenham Court Road

Yasmin Cho

Yasmin Cho's designer-clothing boutique is reminiscent of New York- and European-style exclusive shopping. It is not located at street level and so only people in the know will be browsing there. After being buzzed in, you climb a flight of stairs to a locked door. Finally you enter a large, breezy white room blasting music and atmosphere and full of the season's spectacular clothing from names at the less famous end of the design spectrum.

Cho was born in Sydney and came to London in 1996 to pursue her dream of working in fashion. Stints at *Harper's Bazaar* (in New York) and *Harper's and Queen* (London), plus window dressing at Browns (see page 9.4), confirmed for Cho that she really wanted to be a buyer and have a retail outlet of her own.

August 1999 saw this dream become a reality and while she had not set out to open a shop that was exclusive by its very location, she was always keen to maintain a very high level of customer service that a hidden shop like this was well equipped to provide. It is quite common for customers to come in and spend hours looking and trying on garments, shoes and jewellery before sitting in the comfortable seating area to chat, eat and drink with the ever-affable Cho.

She attributes her immediate success to good PR and a strong client base that she continues to build. This is no doubt aided by the fact that Cho is married to British actor Rufus Sewell. Yet – like with any shop – it is the stock that really keeps customers coming back. Cho's 26 designers come from more than two years of research, attending shows, talking to stylists and reading underground magazines. They hail from her native Australia, the USA, Austria, Belgium and France.

A F van der Vorst's fitted leather trousers for Ruffo Research, Susan Cianciolo's deconstructed skirts and smock shirts and Thimister's evening

wear and long red leather gloves are included in the unusual and eye-catching pieces that hang from industrial rails. Jewellery, bags (beaded by Tracie Anglo and some antique), shoes (by Pierre Hardy and Freddie Stevens for Red) are sourced from Cho's frequent trips to the States and Europe. Alongside the new clothes, there is the odd antique design such as a beaded 1920s flapper-style number with a price tag of £1500.

Cho is definitely not a stop for the bargain hunter (the cheapest item in the shop is a scented nail varnish; a snip at £12), but her customers are paying for much more than the clothes they walk out with. And once inside, Yasmin Cho is a fun and lively space where the concept of retail therapy is carried out fully, with a lot of style and fun to boot.

ADDRESS Level One, 22 Poland Street, London W1 (020 7287 6922)
OPEN Monday to Saturday, 11.00-19.00
UNDERGROUND Oxford Circus

Yasmin Cho

Liberty

Think bales of rich fabrics, jars of sumptuous face lotions, delicate designer clothing and shelves of scented candles and you are probably picturing Liberty. This famous department store was the brainchild of Arthur Lasenby Liberty who was employed at Messrs Farmers and Rogers in Regent Street in 1862. This was the year of the International Exhibition in Kensington which had a section – the first of its kind – devoted to Japan. Farmers and Rogers were already doing considerable trade in Indian shawls at the time, and when the exhibition closed they purchased some of the Japanese stock to form a new Oriental warehouse which they opened adjacent to their main premises. Liberty moved to work in the warehouse and within two years was managing it.

By 1874 Liberty had been managing the Oriental warehouse for ten years. When his request for partnership in the company was rejected he decided to set up on his own. With a £2000 loan from his future father-in-law and a desire to change the style of homeware and fashion, Liberty took on the lease of half a shop at 218a Regent Street; directly opposite Farmers and Rogers. In 1875 when it opened, the store could only afford to employ a 16-year-old girl and a Japanese boy, but within 18 months Liberty had repaid the loan and was selling fabric, ornaments and *objets d'art* from the East and Japan. By 1885 the shop had expanded into 142–144 Regent Street. Soon Liberty was importing from all over Asia and the Middle East; goods from Java, Indochina, India and Persia made Liberty the most fashionable place to shop in London.

Liberty realised that certain Eastern fabrics were too delicate to be used by dressmakers and began to search for English dyers and manufacturers who could experiment in the local production of Eastern-style fabrics and prints. This technique – taking a good idea and adapting it for Western requirements – was to be carried through the whole of the Liberty store.

Liberty

The store's clientele reflected the desirability of the merchandise with famous members of the Pre-Raphaelite movement such as Rosetti, Leighton and Burne-Jones all purchasing goods at Liberty. This kudos put Liberty in a very strong position to be able to commission leading English designers to produce goods under the Liberty banner. Lindsay P Butterfield, who was a leading figure in textiles and Archibald Knox, an established art designer were both prominent figures in the Arts and Crafts and Art Nouveau movements and both of them worked for Liberty. The shop became synonymous with the cutting-edge fashions of the time and made its mark as one of the most prestigious and profitable in London.

Arthur Lasenby Liberty developed the Liberty metalwork and print lines to be distinctive – more than a century later they still are, as is the store itself. Compulsory renovation on the Crown-owned land of bustling Regent Street led Liberty to rebuild East India House during the 1920s. Liberty distinguished his shop from all the other buildings on the street by adding a life-size frieze of figures that gaze onto the street below. As an apt gesture to his original stock line, Liberty also included four Japanese 'lohan' (disciples of Buddha), that sit on a ledge on the first floor on either side of the main entrance.

While the renovations were taking place, Liberty also moved into the Tudor building next door, in order that trading did not have to cease (the two buildings interconnect from inside). The Tudor shop, like East India House, was designed by Edwin T Hall and his son Edwin S Hall. Yet that is where the exterior similarity ends as the latter is very grand and the former is built from the timbers of ships HMS Impregnable and HMS Hindustan. Ever loyal to the Liberty love of detail, Hall made sure that the frontage facing Great Marlborough Street is the same length as the

original Hindustan. Inside, both stores were designed to give a feel of homeliness. Three light wells form the main focus of the building and each is surrounded by smaller rooms, some of which were installed with cosy touches such as fireplaces.

Today Liberty is probably most famous for its textiles. This department was significantly developed in the 1920s when it introduced a range of smaller-scale prints that complemented the fashions of the time and came to be known as 'Liberty Prints'. In the 1960s Jean Muir, Mary Quant, Bill Blass, Cacherel and Yves Saint Laurent all adapted Liberty's 'Lotus Collection' prints for their own demands.

Liberty has managed to remain at the forefront of fashion, style and quality. It maintains a role as a developer of young talent by sponsoring competitions for innovations in pewter, organising a runway show for new British designers, curating design shows in dedicated galleries and engaging in visiting lectureships at key British design colleges. It stocks a vast range of top international designers, luxury goods, jewellery and bodycare products. And although not everything will fall within everyone's price range, visiting Liberty is a fabulous experience in itself, especially around Christmas when creative director Paul Muller initiates a festive decoration theme throughout the store that is matched by few others.

ADDRESS Regent Street, London W1 (020 7734 1234)
WEBSITE www.liberty-of-london.com
OPEN Monday to Wednesday, 10.00–18.30; Thursday, 10.00–20.00;
Friday, Saturday, 10.00–19.00
UNDERGROUND Oxford Circus

MAC

Make-up Artist's Cosmetics began as the brainchild of Frank Toskan and the late Frank Angelo in Toronto in 1985. In 1993 the Canadian company opened its first international location at Harvey Nichols in Knightsbridge.

MAC always had an edge on more traditional make-up brands because its products are used by so many professionals. Make-up artists working on films, photo-shoots and fashion shows were the first to use MAC and introduced the brand to the celebrities they worked with. And celebrity word-of-mouth meant that the company quickly received press coverage and wide recognition.

MAC stores and outlets follow specific design standards and London's most recently opened branch in Kensington (Unit 4, 28a Kensington Church Street, w8), is an excellent example. Powders, foundations, lipsticks, glitters and eye-shadows are openly displayed and easy to sample. MAC was one of the first brands to encourage their customers to try everything before they buy. Staff are always on hand in the stores with cleansers and make-up removers to get rid of anything you try on or suggest new items as they come in.

Although MAC does not use one face to personify its products, the stunning 6-foot-plus black drag-queen Ru Paul is affiliated with the MAC Aids Fund and Viva Glam lipstick, one of the main money-generating tools of the fund. Almost one and a half million Viva Glam lipsticks have been sold, raising more than $12 million. MAC also rewards the eco-conscious – customers receive free lipsticks when they return MAC casings for recycling.

ADDRESS 28 Foubert's Place, London w1 (020 7534 9222)
OPEN Monday to Wednesday, Saturday, 10.00–18.30; Thursday, 10.00–19.30; Friday, 12.00–17.30
UNDERGROUND Oxford Circus

Muji

Muji first opened in the United Kingdom in 1991, and immediately caught the attention of all who visited its west Soho branch. This, the first international branch of a huge Japanese chain, stood out from other shops because of its singular attitude to its products and the way it sold them.

Muji is an abbreviation of *mujirushi ryohin* which, literally translated, means 'no-brand quality goods'. None of Muji's products carries a label and all are made from high-quality raw materials with an emphasis on natural materials and colours.

With their neutrally designed and coloured setting, visiting a Muji store is a rather Zen experience. Rows of earthenware crockery and bamboo chopsticks appeal to those who like clean living and modern design. Storage units, both stationary and portable, made from steel, plywood, canvas, polypropylene, or cardboard are versatile and practical. Utility products such as buckets, hangers and even toilet brushes mean that you can have the Muji ethic carried through every element of home living. Muji clothes, available in plain colours, are easy to wear and easy to care for.

And this focus has proved extremely successful; Muji plans to open 50 stores in Europe by 2003. The Tottenham Court Road branch is the UK's largest, but all Muji stores stock the same products and – apart from the clothing lines – little changes from season to season, ensuring that staple favourites never go out of style. And after all, if you were never about label-conscious fashion in the first place, how can you go out of it?

ADDRESS 6 Tottenham Court Road, London W1 (020 7323 2208)
OPEN Monday to Wednesday, Saturday, 10.00–20.00; Thursday, Friday, 10.00–20.30; Sunday 12.00–18.00
UNDERGROUND Tottenham Court Road

The Pinneal Eye

The Pinneal Eye is the all-seeing spiritual third eye of which the French philosopher George Bataille wrote in *Against Architecture*. Yuko Yabuki and Nicola Formichetti (the former is a Japanese woman and the latter an Italian-Japanese man), opened their insightful vision point in the form of a shop on 1 July 1998. It immediately commanded attention from passers-by, not because of the name (which is only identifiable on the price tags; not on the actual storefront), but because the ground-level entrance opens up a huge amount of space. It leads straight on to a gangway that becomes a staircase directing customers to the basement floor where all the merchandise is displayed. Yabuki and Formichetti utilise this space like a gallery and hang strangely attired mannequins from the ceiling into it. Every month the display is changed – small brightly dressed dolls and hanging vegetables have worked equally well as crowd-stoppers.

Yabuki and Formichetti wanted to create a space to show the work of young designers. Their stock is definitely more edge – some of it verging on unwearable – than some of their competitors, but Yabuki and Formichetti win hands down when it comes to innovation. Apart from the clothes, they also stock shoes, accessories and a healthy and eclectic range of Japanese and fashion magazines and fanzines.

The Pinneal Eye is Yabuki's second commercial venture in the area. She previously opened a Japanese accessory shop, Kokon To Zai. It was there that she met Formichetti, then studying architecture, and they decided to branch out into the fickle world of fashion. But if anyone can predict the future of fashion, surely it will be The Pinneal Eye.

ADDRESS 49 Broadwick Street, London W1 (020 7434 2567)
OPEN Monday to Saturday 11.00–19.00
UNDERGROUND Oxford Circus

W I

Ozwald Boateng

Things are not quite what they seem at Ozwald Boateng. A sleekly cut suit in a conservative fabric is what you see at first glance. Look inside and an acid green, lemon yellow, blood crimson or lavender lilac lining will mark out the wearer (and he makes suits for both men and women), to be more than what first meets the eye.

Boateng himself is striking for a bespoke tailor located at the south of Savile Row. Tall, black and lean, he could be one of his own runway models. It is the carnival of what Boateng creates that marks him out from the more traditional tailors of Savile Row. He has achieved this style with some very clever tailoring techniques. Angled pockets which enhance shape, high-fastening jackets, tapered trousers and concealed buttons give his creations a line that is sleek and a look that is slick.

The business that he had been building to encompass the shop and two annual ready-to-wear collections alongside the bespoke service was sadly affected by the recession in the Far East in early 1998. Boateng was forced to liquidate his original company, but has bounced back on track with renewed vigour over the past two years. Not only did he manage to retain the shop throughout the crisis but has subsequently opened the first couture house for men in the United Kingdom. 83 Wimpole Street, W1 has been home to both Boateng and his design headquarters since summer 1999. The building has been decorated with brightly coloured carpeting and murals and paint effects by artist Kevin Allison. You will not be disappointed if you take the time to examine what you see a little more closely.

ADDRESS 9 Vigo Street, London W1 (0207 734 6868)
WEBSITE www.bespokecouture.com
OPEN Monday to Saturday, 10.00–18.00
UNDERGROUND Piccadilly Circus

Browns

For more than 30 years Browns has kept a fairly low profile while maintaining a very high reputation for stocking ultra-fashionable labels through its ever-multiplying outlets on the anomaly that is South Molton Street. Like many of London's quieter pedestrian streets, South Molton was for many years a quiet offshoot from the hustle and bustle of Oxford Street. It housed unusual boutiques and a Drugstore that survives and sells some of the cheapest make-up in the capital. But it was this same proximity to heavy shopper traffic that has more recently caused South Molton Street to turn into a walkway with all the usual high-street branches present and accountable.

But back in 1970 nobody really knew where South Molton Street was and the Burnstein family were in the process of purchasing a fashion boutique at number 27 from Sir William Piggot-Brown. They kept the name (Browns is after all, slightly more generic than Burnstein), and the stock description, and proceeded to grow the business into London's most successful multi-label outlet outside of the huge department stores.

Browns has overseen the sale of clothes by Calvin Klein, Giorgio Armani, Missoni, Norma Kamali, Azzedine Alaia, Donna Karen and Sonia Rykiel in their shops over the past three decades. Sections of the stores are dedicated to each designer and Romeo Gigli (for himself), Michael Gabellini (for Jil Sander) and Rei Kawakubo (for Comme des Garçons) have all specially designed mini 'outlets' to reflect their clothes and visions.

The variety and quantity of stock at Browns has long made it a celebrity magnet. The staff are trained to take great care with customers and are discrete to the point where they will shut the shop or make specific behind-closed-door appointments with certain people. Perhaps surprisingly, this has not turned Browns into a snobby elitist establishment. As it acquired

numbers 23, 24, 25, 26 and eventually 38–39 and 50, the space has been used both to expand the number of designers whose clothes are stocked and to open other boutiques – Browns Living, Browns Label, Browns Labels for Less and Browns Focus.

Browns Labels for Less replaced Browns Own Label at number 50 and Browns Focus, which opened in 1997 at number 38, is the shop aimed at the street-fashion-conscious style-tribe. These two outlets in particular are aimed at a young clientele and this is apparent in the prices and styles of the garments.

ADDRESS 23–27 South Molton Street, London W1 (020 7514 0000)
OPEN Monday to Saturday, 10.00–18.30; Thursday, 10.00–19.00
UNDERGROUND Bond Street

Nicole Farhi Home

Nicole Farhi has been designing clothes for more than two decades. Born in Nice, she studied fashion in Paris but came over to London in the early 1970s to work on the international high-street label French Connection with her then-husband Stephen Marks. In 1983 they launched the Farhi label and have since built that into a business that comprises eight London stores, a restaurant called Nicole's (in the basement of the flagship store at 158 New Bond Street, W1), and a shop in New York (which similarly features her restaurant on the lower-ground floor).

In 1999 one of her passions found its home at Nicole Farhi Home. Her hand-picked collection of antiques (many of which are sourced by Farhi herself on trips back to her native France) sits alongside (if not on), a range of contemporary table- and bedware, linen, crockery and glassware. Tables, mirrors, books and candles allow the Farhi sensibility to infiltrate more of the customer's life than just what they wear. Total lifestyle visions are fast becoming popular with designers who have succeeded in one field. Turnover is singular and rapid, so it is always worth dropping in. Either before or after you have visited Nicole's in your latest Farhi outfit.

ADDRESS 17 Clifford Street, London W1 (020 7494 9051)
OPEN Monday to Saturday, 10.00–18.00; Thursday, 10.00–19.00
UNDERGROUND Piccadilly Circus

Richard James

The fact that this shop is located on Savile Row presupposes that Richard James is a tailor. For almost two centuries Savile Row has been home to fine bespoke tailoring – it was here in the Regency period that the look of the English gentleman that endures to this day was fashioned.

Since 1922 when he started the company with Sean Dixon, Richard James has upheld that impeccable look, but restyled it with a modern twist. His fabrics seem inspired more by dizzying Bridget Riley canvases than the conservative pinstripes available from his neighbours. Vibrant colours, eccentric prints and clever cuts are what make James's suits stand out from the crowd. Fuschia tartan and indigo spot prints make an unlikely combination but surprisingly knit together in his slick designs.

Of course it is these eccentricities that have attracted customers who raise the James profile. Jarvis Cocker, David Linley, Elton John and Christian Lacroix are all fans and have worn James's suits for photoshoots as well as in everyday life. Which is essentially the defining quality of James's work: that it will mark its wearers out from the crowd, without encroaching on their individual sense of style.

ADDRESS 31 Savile Row, London W1 (020 7434 0605)
WEBSITE www.richardjames.co.uk
OPEN Monday to Friday, 11.00–18.00; Saturday, 10.00–18.00
UNDERGROUND Piccadilly Circus

w1

Ralph Lauren

Truly a flagship store, Ralph Lauren has spread his high-quality products over seven floors and 24,000 square feet of retail space. Mahogany panelling, working fireplaces and a collection of fine art and photography on the walls give the impression of a wealthy home on the Eastern seaboard – one perhaps not dissimilar to how you would imagine Brooklyn born-and-bred Lauren's might be.

This branch opened in May of 1999 and replaced an older and smaller version that had been located up the road on Bond Street. Thierry Despont designed the store to include lounging areas with comfy chairs in order to accommodate tired shoppers and effectively increase the time they spend shopping here.

The store houses all the Ralph Lauren lines. His clothes, be they formal or sportswear, share a style that is as classic as it is fashionable. Rich textiles and clean lines have kept Lauren's clothes in high esteem with a huge international following and he has cleverly developed diffusion lines such as Polo and household goods that mean his label can define more of his customer's lives than just what they wear. Sporting goods, fragrances, candles and toiletries have driven the Lauren name to equal high-end rather than high-street retailing. With a shop to match the fashion and superb quality of everything he produces, Lauren cannot fail to impress.

ADDRESS 143 New Bond Street, London W1 (020 7491 4967)
OPEN Monday to Saturday, 10.00–18.00; Thursday, 10.00–19.00
UNDERGROUND Green Park

Alexander McQueen

Lee Alexander McQueen is one of the UK's hottest designers. Ever since he bared the bottoms of his models in 'bumsters' on the catwalk in the 1995's 'Highland Rape' show, McQueen has kept his profile high and his trousers cut low.

The path that led him to open his own store at the end of 1999 has been long and hard, but his work paid off when in 1996 McQueen was appointed head of Givenchy. He designs for the French couture house while retaining his own label in London, where he has also remained based.

McQueen left school at 16 with just one O-Level (in art). His social background – working-class, east London, homosexual son of a taxi driver – did not make it easy to pursue his dream of designing clothes. But replying to an advert for the position of tailor's apprentice at Anderson and Sheppard of Savile Row gave him two and a half years of valuable cutting experience. This was followed by a year of trouser cutting at Gieves and Hawkes before McQueen moved on to the theatrical costumiers Bermans and Nathans. It was at the first that he famously wrote 'I'm a cunt' in the lining of a jacket that was destined for Prince Charles. In 1992 he graduated from St Martin's School of Art with an MA in fashion.

This, the first McQueen shop, has given him an opportunity to bring his total vision to the public. Designed by Azman Owens, a young Turkish-American architectural practice, the focus of the shop is an incredible installation tank made of thick glass jutting out of the front window. The scene inside changes from season to season to reflect McQueen's current collections. The first featured a blizzard-induced snowstorm, lit by ultra-violet bulbs on the floor and ceiling of the tank. Inside, the mannequins wore garments from the corresponding autumn/

Alexander McQueen

winter 1999–2000 collection. Called 'Overlook', it was inspired by Stanley Kubrick's film *The Shining*.

The store itself is innovatively versatile with metal panels that double as frames and move between suspended garment rails. The changing rooms are made of glass that frosts up by itself when customers enter. Their dual use as garment storage space gives the shop a functional Meccano-set feel.

ADDRESS 47 Conduit Street, London W1 (020 7734 2340)
OPEN Monday to Saturday, 10.00–18.00
UNDERGROUND Oxford Circus

Issey Miyake

Perhaps more than any other designer, Issey Miyake has blurred the distinctions between fashion and art and art and fashion. Much of his work is instantly recognisable even to those who aren't extremely label conscious. This is largely due to the Japanese designer's fearlessness in pushing the boundaries of clothing and pioneering textiles and shapes. Miyake's work is versatile, wearable and suits an incredible range of body sizes. Its egalitarianism has made it popular with people all over the world, regardless of age, sex, shape, size or social status.

Born in Hiroshima in 1938, Miyake studied at the Ecole de la Chambre Syndicale de la Couture Parisienne and worked in Paris and New York for Guy Laroche and Hubert de Givenchy before he opened his own house, Miyake Design Studio (MDS) in Tokyo in 1970. This hothouse of innovation has launched two men's and two women's collections a year since 1973 (which are always shown in Paris), and is responsible today for the Issey Miyake line, the revolutionary Pleats Please line that was launched in 1993, and most recently his latest baby, the A-POC range.

Miyake has contributed work to many major museum exhibitions over the past 30 years – 'A Piece of Cloth – Issey Miyake in Museum' (Seibu Museum of Art, Tokyo, 1977), 'Issey Miyake Bodyworks: Fashion without Taboos' (Victoria & Albert Museum, London, 1985), 'Energies – 1990' (Stedelijk Museum, Amsterdam, 1990), and 'Addressing the Century: 100 years of Art and Fashion' (Hayward Gallery, London, 1998) to name just four. Miyake handed over his men's range to Naoki Takizawa in 1993. His women's range followed in 1999 (the two have been collaborating for years), and while he remains creative director of all that emerges from MDS, he will focus on A-POC, a name derived from his 1977 exhibition 'A Piece of Cloth'. The idea that clothing can literally

Issey Miyake

be made from a single piece of cloth has resulted in a very experimental project with unlimited possibilities using highly developed technologies.

Pleats Please was launched in 1993. The range is wrinkle-free, machine-washable, incredibly versatile, flattering – and an avant-garde fashion statement. Now A-POC looks set to follow in its footsteps and – as with Pleats Please – Miyake hopes to open an A-POC store in London in the near future to sell this range.

ADDRESS 52 Conduit Street, London W1/20 Brook Street, London W1
(020 7851 4620/020 7495 2306)
WEBSITE www.pleatsplease.com
OPEN Monday to Saturday, 10.00–18.00
UNDERGROUND Oxford Circus/Bond Street

w1

Selfridges

Its mission statement is 'to be the best and most exciting department store in Europe'. More than half a million square feet of retail space, five floors linked by escalators, the largest beauty hall in Europe and a £99 million refurbishment that ended at the start of the new millennium are making this a reality.

ADDRESS 400 Oxford Street, London W1 (020 7629 1234)
WEBSITE www.selfridges.co.uk
OPEN Monday to Wednesday, Saturday, 10.00–19.00; Thursday, Friday, 10.00–20.00; Sunday, 12.00–18.00
UNDERGROUND Bond Street

Spymaster

This is the shop in which every child whose imagination has been captured by James Bond movies wishes to choose his birthday presents. Spymaster sells the most extensive range of 'communications and surveillance' equipment that you are ever likely to come across unless you work for a government organisation.

'Communications' at Spymaster means tape recorders hidden in books, belts, and bags, that can record up to six hours of speech. 'Surveillance' is microphones and cameras hidden in clocks, wall-sockets, smoke-detectors, watches and calculators. And the exciting world of counter-surveillance means devices such as the '7000 Encrypted Telephone' which prevents phone tapping, and pens that double as bug detectors.

Binoculars with night vision, cameras and torches appeal to the same customers who come in for bullet proof vests, camouflage creams and flare kits. There are survival kits and books on how to use them plus an intriguing range of books with titles that include *How to Disappear Completely* and *Methods of Disguise* (presumably they *are* intriguing – Spymaster employs the clever marketing ploy of sealing their books so you can't flick through them without purchasing).

Spymaster is very popular with wealthy foreigners – hence the 'Gulf 3 Camel Racing Communications System' and the 'Desert Ranger Falcon Tracking System'. The store stays open slightly later in the summer to accommodate its nomadic clientele.

ADDRESS 3 Portman Square, London W1 (020 7486 3885)
WEBSITE www.spymaster.co.uk
OPEN winter: Monday to Friday, 9.30–18.00; summer: Monday to Friday, 9.30–18.30; Saturday 10.00–17.00
UNDERGROUND Bond Street

Versace

Glamour, glamour, glamour. Both Gianni Versace and the fashion house were never about understatement. Even Versace's death in 1997 – at the hands of a serial killer in Miami – made headline news all over the world.

But the Versace family are used to this. Gianni's sister Donnatella took over the design house and kept up the friendships with all the A-grade celebs. Madonna, Sting, Jon Bon Jovi, Elton John, Liz Hurley, and every supermodel worth her weight in Versace jewellery are patrons of this Italian *uber*-fashion house.

The Versace shop on New Bond Street is a statement. The 1025 square metres were designed by Laboratorio Associati and form the largest 'jeans' store in the world. Five floors house the Versus line, Versace Jeans Couture, Versace Sport, Versace Intensive and Young Versace.

Neon and glass were key in the fitting of this very impressive store. Illuminated glass floors containing video screens give an impression of light and movement between the levels. A glass elevator and staircase link the floors that are personed by attractive Versace-clad staff. The third and fourth floors have been named 'The Black Suite' and, as a tribute to the dead designer, they take clothes from all the collections but display only the black version.

ADDRESS 113–117 New Bond Street, London W1 (020 7355 2700)
OPEN Monday to Saturday, 10.00–18.00; Thursday, 10.00–19.00
UNDERGROUND Bond Street

Vivienne Westwood

The doyenne of designers and the countess of couture, Vivienne Westwood has long been a force to be reckoned with. Back in 1971 at the age of 30 she opened a shop at 430 King's Road. Subsequently, the shop's stock and name went through a series of transformations that reflected Westwood's influences. 'Let it Rock' sold rock'n'roll clothing when hippies were still in fashion. 'Too fast to live, too young to die' sold clothes for rockers; zoot suits and T-shirts with slogans and zips and chains. Westwood was one of the pioneers of punk fashion during her relationship with Sex Pistols manager Malcolm McLaren and sold clothing through this shop under the banners of 'Sex' and then 'World's End', the name that finally stuck.

Westwood, however, moved on and her Pirate collection was shown in 1981 at Olympia. She opened a second shop called 'Nostalgia of Mud' which closed at the end of 1984, the year that also saw the end of her collaboration with McLaren. But by that time Westwood's star was in the ascendant. In 1982 she was the first British designer since Mary Quant to show in Paris since and in 1984 she showed her collection in Tokyo with Hanae Mori, Calvin Klein, Claude Montana and Gianfranco Ferre at the 'Best of Five'.

Westwood has four labels in production: Vivienne Westwood Gold Label (the couture line that is shown on the catwalk), Red Label by Vivienne Westwood (the diffusion line which is also made in Italy), MAN (her menswear line, launched in 1990), and Anglomania (Westwood's casual line, launched in 1998).

The shop on Conduit Street is one of three in London. World's End still exists and there is another at 6 Davies Street, also in W1. Conduit Street is the newest and the flagship store, covering three floors with Westwood's designs for both men and women.

Vivienne Westwood

   Much of Westwood's individuality stems from her embracing of all that is native to her. Her collections have resembled Elizabethan costumes, complete with full skirts, bustles, bodices and the famous bust-enhancing corsets. She created her own tartan for the 'Anglomania' collection of autumn/winter 1993/94. Like Westwood herself, the clothes are about statement, drama and effect and do not suit people with small personalities.

ADDRESS 44 Conduit Street, London w1 (020 7287 3188)
OPEN Monday to Saturday, 10.00–18.00; Thursday, 10.00–19.00
UNDERGROUND Oxford Circus

piccadilly

Geo F. Trumper

A royal warrant was awarded by Queen Victoria soon after Trumper's establishment in 1875, an honour that was repeated through the five subsequent reigns. Trumper's was one of the very first exclusive barber's shops for gentlemen in London when he opened his Curzon Street premises. His reputation both as a barber and as a formulator of distinctive high-quality colognes and pomades grew rapidly and turned Trumper into a sought-after brand name.

When Trumper retired the business was taken on by his daughter. There being no immediate family to take the reins after her, Trumper's came under the supervision of Ivan Bersch in the mid-twentieth century. Bersch added more products to Trumper's traditional lines, while maintaining the standard of excellence relied upon by the distinguished clientele.

These days, the range of pomades, creams and men's toiletries leaves nothing to be desired. Lazy Scalp is a conditioner to help stimulate hair growth; Green Floreka is a dressing that holds hair in place with oil. No gentleman should ever be without his West Indian Extract of Limes hair cream that provides body with non-greasy holding power, or the shampoos and conditioners that range from egg and lanolin to nettle, willow and thyme. Soaps and shower gels merely complement the huge choice of shaving creams and aftershaves. Blocks of alum, the original antiseptic aftershave, provide an alternative to Royal Cologne, Spanish Leather Cologne and even Eau de Quinine.

These are only the disposable products. Trumper's houses the most extensive (and sometimes expensive) range of shaving stands, brushes and razors (double-sided, cartridge or open) that you are ever likely to lay eyes on. Moustache, beard and nostril requisites, manicure sets, as well as hair, clothes and body brushes are also available.

Geo F. Trumper

Providing his customers with an array of leather-bound steel hip flasks and walking sticks, Trumper ensured that they left the premises in a state that was never less than immaculate.

The barber service is still available in the bowels of the traditionally furnished shop. Little do passers-by on well-to-do Jermyn Street realise that below the very pavement upon which they tread men are being scrubbed, shaved and cut, before emerging, the very picture of modern English gentlemen.

ADDRESS 20 Jermyn Street, London SW1 (0207 734 1370/6553)
OPEN Monday to Friday, 9.00–18.00; Saturday 9.00–17.00
TUBE Piccadilly Circus

piccadilly

Georgina von Etzdorf

Although those fantastic, sought-after scarves are sold under one name, Georgina von Etzdorf is really the collaborative effort of three people. Von Etzdorf herself has always been the artistic focus of the company, but she has been working alongside Martin Simcock and Jonathan Docherty since it was founded in 1981. Von Etzdorf and Simcock, now head of research and development, had met while they were studying textile design at Camberwell School of Art; Docherty, now managing director, had known Simcock since their teenage years.

Von Etzdorf and Simcock began with a £500 grant from the Crafts Council and some rudimentary printing equipment. They experimented with dyes, fabrics and printing methods and the results were stunning. Worn by the likes of Mick Jagger, David Bowie, Meryl Streep and Princess Diana (Donald Campbell used von Etzdorf's printed-wool poppy design for one of her dresses), the popularity of the designs grew and grew. By 1986 they had opened the shop in the Burlington Arcade and were making shoes, gloves and belts. By the end of the millennium von Etzdorf had launched her own home-furnishings collection, made her name available through 400 outlets in 21 countries (including Barney's in New York), opened – and then closed – shops on Sloane Street and Ledbury Road. She even designed a rug collection for Christopher Farr (see page 5.12). Diversification and experimentation obviously do not scare Georgina von Etzdorf. The company maintains its position at at the establishment edge of British design.

ADDRESS 1–2 Burlington Arcade, London W1 (020 7409 7789)
OPEN Monday to Saturday, 9.30–18.00
UNDERGROUND Green Park

Waterstone's

This, perhaps Europe's largest bookstore, opened in autumn 1999, and just might represent the future of bookselling. Forget poky, dusty and dingy little shops, Waterstone's on Piccadilly is seven floors of retail therapy, restaurants, bars and events. It is open until 11 at night and there are comfy, modern chairs positioned throughout the store where browsers can sit and read for hours without ever having to buy. It is fashionable and cool, full of fashionable and cool people all reading or eating or drinking or smoking (in the refreshment areas), or chatting. It is brightly lit and easy to use.

Until recently this listed building housed Simpson's. Alexander Simpson, a successful menswear manufacturer, commissioned the design from Joseph Emberton. Influenced by the Bauhaus, he made innovative use of chromium plate, natural light and clear glass throughout the building. Non-reflective curved windows and shadowless lighting attracted the eyes of passers-by and the input of leading European designers. Bauhaus legend Laszlo Moholy-Nagy responded by taking a personal role in the displays for Simpson's goods and managed to install three aeroplanes into the opening displays on the fifth floor. When it opened on 29 April 1936, the shop offered an astounding range of services. Apart from Simpson's clothes there was a pet store, a theatre-ticket concession, a golf range, a sportswear shop, a branch of Thomas Cook's travel agents, a barber, a flower shop, a tobacconist, a milliner and several restaurants and snack bars.

Waterstone's has made effective use of the massive space. Apart from a juice bar, café and restaurant and lounge bar (that serves alcohol and is full of attractive people), there are internet stations, an out-of-print book search service and a personal shopping service. The entire sixth floor is given over to events and an exhibition space to be used by artists and

writers. There is an ongoing programme of authors' talks and book-signings and children are well catered for.

In Simpson's (the original shop's signage has been installed on the wall of the sixth floor), Waterstone's is attempting to strike out in a new direction. Faced by the undeniable threat to traditional bookselling posed by e-commerce, it has made a bookshop into a fashionable hang-out.

ADDRESS 203–206 Piccadilly, London W1 (020 7851 2400)
WEBSITE www.waterstones.co.uk
OPEN Monday to Saturday, 8.30–23.00; Sunday, 12.00–18.00
UNDERGROUND Piccadilly Circus

st christopher's place/
marylebone

Aveda

During the 1960s and 1970s Horst Rechelbacher experimented with plants in his kitchen in Minneapolis and concocted his first batch of pure plant shampoo. Since then his name has become synonymous with the manufacturing of cosmetic and environmental care products made from freshly distilled plant and flower essences. In 1978 Rechelbacher began selling the products under the Aveda name, which was derived from the term 'Ayurvedic', the ancient Hindu science of longevity.

More than 20 years later the brand has established a worldwide reputation. The company sources the flower and plant base of its products from all over the world and is keen to eliminate the use of petrochemicals and synthetics from consumer goods.

All of this is apparent on a stroll through any Aveda shop or salon. London's Aveda Institute is a lovely example of this. Part of the shop – located in a former high-street post office – has been given over to a café called 'Love', intended to enhance the social and family aspects of shopping at Aveda. As an 'institute' rather than just a shop, they have also dedicated the basement as an area for staff to train and workshops to be held.

ADDRESS 28–29 Marylebone High Street, London W1 (020 7224 3157)
WEBSITE www.aveda.com
OPEN Monday to Friday, 9.30–19.00; Saturday, 9.00–18.00
UNDERGROUND Baker Street

Mint

Mint was opened by Jordanian-born Lina Kanafani in December 1998. She originally came to London to study biochemistry but later switched professional directions by writing the first Middle Eastern diet cookbook.

Kanafani refurbished a hotel on the Fulham Road and was making pyjamas and bags that she sold through Liberty before the plans for Mint were born. She had the vision to convert a cute South African wine shop into a design Mecca. Kanafani has kept the alcoves used previously as wine cellars and stocked them with furniture. The shop's ambience has something of the church or mosque about it and the light, scent and space all contribute to this quality.

Spread over two floors are fishing baskets, sieves made from animal skins and recycled rubber products scattered across the floor and in the alcoves. Kanafani regularly travels back to the Middle East and rescues Bedouin bags, copper pots and camel shawls to add to the display. Yet it would be wrong to think that the shop is full of ethnic junk as Mint is fast becoming a springboard for young European designers. Two recent discoveries (both French) are Christine Goumot, who crafts solid zinc tables, and Anne Chaudeville, who makes gossip cushions – clear plastic cushions stuffed full of shredded paper from the pages of gossip magazines. This amusing idea comes in two sizes so you can choose the relevant cushion depending on how much you like to talk about others.

Old and new, modern and traditional, Mint acknowledges its roots but has set a course for the future. Its philosophy should definitely be tasted.

ADDRESS 70 Wigmore Street, London W1 (020 7224 4406)
OPEN Monday to Saturday, 10.30–18.30; Thursday, 10.30–19.30
UNDERGROUND Bond Street

st christopher's place/marylebone

V V Rouleaux

This posh-sounding name is simply that – a posh-sounding name. V V Rouleaux is not a French madam living a life of luxury – she is in fact Annabel Lewis who formerly owned a florist's shop in the nondescript London suburb of Parsons Green. But her eye for the finer things did enhance her interest in frippery. Visits to department stores proved less than satisfying; none of them stocked the range of ribbons, fringes, feathers and tassels she was seeking. In 1990 Lewis opened up the most divine trimmings shop in the whole of London: V V Rouleaux.

More than 5000 ribbons line the shelves of this two-storey shop on Marylebone High Street. Ribbons with beads, ribbons with animal patterns, tartan ribbons, gorgette ribbons, silk ribbons, cotton ribbons, velvet ribbons. If they don't have it they'll tell you how to make it for yourself and the staff are happy to help with ideas for customising clothes and cushions. But the real beauty of V V Rouleaux is that you never know what you will find there and you will probably be inspired by all of it.

ADDRESS 6 Marylebone High Street, London W1 (020 7224 5179)
OPEN Monday to Saturday, 9.30–18.00
UNDERGROUND Bond Street

Skandium

Scandium (the correct spelling in English) is a costly and rare base metal which has no particular use, as yet. Skandium – the shop – is filled with costly (yet affordable), rare (anywhere but Scandinavia), basic metal and glassware, furniture, lights, crockery, jewellery and books that have many particular uses.

The store – the only all-Scandinavian design shop outside the northern land mass – opened in September 1999. It is the result of the collaborative efforts of Finnish photographer Christina Schmidt, Swedish fashion retailer Magnus Englund and Danish stockbroker Christopher Seiden-faden.

Economic and political history is reflected in the style of each country represented here. Generally, Scandinavian design is functional and prac-tical, reflecting the socialist atmosphere of the past century. Traditionally, the designs of Finns and Swedes, situated more to the north, have been sparser than those of relatively opulent, less-isolated Denmark.

Skandium has sourced a range that is innovative, stylish, inspiring and steeped in history. Arne Jacobsen's Swan chair, designed in 1957 for the SAS Royal Copenhagen Hotel (£1200; £2180 in leather), is a classic, as is Paul Henningsen's (for Louis Poulson) Artichoke lampshade (1958). Its size meant that this was originally intended for more public spaces, but as homes have grown, the vegetable-shaped fronds and soft light effect are seen almost as frequently as his Snowball and PH5 lamps in Scandinavian homes.

The store is spread over two floors with white walls, high ceilings and stark light filtering through two huge windows. A whole section is given over to chairs. Verner Panton's eponymous chair sits next to Poul M Volther's Corona chair of 1962. The latter's unusual shape (three curved cushions and a seat attached to a visible main frame that swivels on a

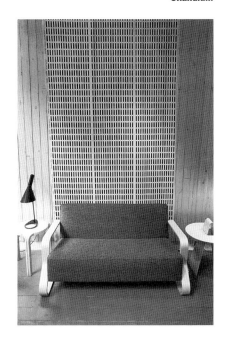

steel base) was inspired by time-lapse photography developed to capture solar eclipses. The Bowie chair produced by Claesson, Koivisto and Rune in 1998 and the very different Nandin chair by Hans Peter Weidmann for Artek (also 1998) are both made in bent birchwood. The wide Atlas easy chair by Johannes Foersom and Peter Hiort Lorensen is covered in stripy upholstery, while the linking Wedding Stools by Thomas Sandell for Asplund are far simpler but arguably just as striking.

Glassware by Tapio Wirkkala (1915–85) represents classic Finnish design (multi-talented, he was responsible not only for glassware, but also for banknote design, utility graphics, and even the Finlandia vodka bottle). Goran Hongell (1902–73), Kaj Franck (1911–89) and Aino and Alvar Aalto were also pioneer glassware designers.

The designers mentioned here represent a fraction of those whose work Skandium has on show. Scandinavia is renowned for the beauty its twentieth-century design has brought to everyday life. Scandium is a one-stop shop for worshippers of this simple vision.

ADDRESS 72 Wigmore Street, London W1 (020 7935 2077)
WEBSITE www.skandium.com
OPEN Monday to Saturday, 10.00–18.30; Sunday, 12.00–17.00
UNDERGROUND Bond Street

covent garden

The Bead Shop

More than 5000 varieties of bead are waiting to be strung into necklaces, sewn on to handbags or simply admired in this shop that started as a tiny outlet on Neal Street way back in 1977. Founder Parveen Khan soon found that the demand for her beads was spreading far and wide and by 1979 she had established a wholesale business and mail-order catalogue alongside the shop.

Since then The Bead Shop has distributed its phenomenal range throughout the USA, Australia, Europe and Japan. What was once a gap in the market has now become far more competitive with accessory and cheap jewellery shops opening up everywhere. The Bead Shop has maintained its pioneering position by keeping costs low and, more importantly, expanding its range of beads.

Coloured and speckled glass, Venetian glass, lead crystal, embroidered and Chinese porcelain varieties are all to be found nestling in wooden boxes and ready to fit on to a leather cord. Silver and gold, semi-precious stones and beads shaped like fish, lanterns or animals are all on display. The Bead Shop will provide everything other than imagination when it comes to crafting jewellery on your own.

ADDRESS 21a Tower Street, London WC2 (020 7240 0931)
OPEN Monday, 13.00–18.00; Tuesday–Friday, 10.30–18.00;
Saturday 11.30–17.00
UNDERGROUND Covent Garden or Leicester Square

Koh Samui

The original Koh Samui is an exotic island off the coast of Thailand; Covent Garden's is a clothes shop full of designer treasures. It was opened by Talita Zoe and Paul Sexton in the mid 1990s and their success in spotting, supporting and stocking young designers meant that they were able to add a second store (28 Lowndes Street, SW1) to their stable at the end of 1998.

Zoe and Sexton spend much of their time searching out new talent and were pivotal in helping the careers of Christa Davies (very delicate and beautiful skirts, cardigans, coats and dresses, prettily adorned with ribbons and *faux* flowers), Makus Lupfer (synthetic textiles complementing abstract designs), and Ruti Danan (pretty lace dresses).

Bigger brands such as Missoni, Clements Ribiero and Emma Hope are stocked these days, but Koh Samui's roots and loyalty remain with young British designers whose work they continue to source and promote.

ADDRESS 65–67 Upper St Martin's Lane, London WC2 (020 7240 4280)
OPEN Monday to Wednesday, Saturday, 10.00–18.30; Thursday, Friday, 10.00–19.00
UNDERGROUND Leicester Square

Neal's Yard Remedies

It was in 1981 that Romy Fraser felt inspired by the natural remedies that she had seen in French pharmacies and decided that it was time to open something similar in the UK.

Set in the mayhem of tourist-ridden Covent Garden and Neal Street (once a quiet street hiding one-off boutiques; now infested with high-street chain branches), Neal's Yard has kept to its natural roots. It is home to several tiny shops, healthfood bars, a bakery and a massage unit, as well as Fraser's Remedies.

From the start Neal's Yard Remedies stocked a wide range of herbs, essential oils and homeopathic medicines. Today many of these products and their approach are commonplace, but in the early 1980s Neal's Yard was a pioneer in educating the public; experienced staff could explain to customers why they should take Echinacea Goldenseal rather than anti-biotics or St John's Wort rather than prescription antidepressants. To further this mission, Fraser co-wrote *Natural Healing for Women* and *Neal's Yard Remedies*, an A to Z of ailments and their corresponding homeopathic, herbal and aromatherapy treatments. Fraser set up a free advice hotline in 1998 and is also responsible for workshops in some of the Neal's Yard Remedy outlets around the country; aromatherapy, Indian head massage and flower remedies are some of the most popular.

Neal's Yard Remedies remains true to it natural roots. It makes products – beautifully packaged in trademark blue glass – that care for people who care about themselves, the environment and each other.

ADDRESS 15 Neal's Yard, London WC2 (020 7379 7222)
OPEN Monday, 10.00–18.00; Tuesday to Friday, 10.00–19.00; Saturday, 10.00–17.30; Sunday, 11.00–17.00
UNDERGROUND Covent Garden

James Smith and Sons Umbrellas

The first umbrella arrived in Europe – care of Jonas Hanway – from Asia in the mid to late 1700s. Smith and Sons Umbrellas has a similarly long history. Since 1830 the descendants of James Smith have been selling umbrellas and walking sticks. They have been trading from the same premises at Hazlewood House since the son of the original Mr Smith (also called James), opened the shop there in 1857. It was also during the 19th Century that the umbrella trade really expanded. In 1847 Samuel Fox invented the revolutionary steel frame which had the positive result of being much lighter and more compact than the previous umbrellas that had been designed from cane and whale bone.

At Hazlewood House a vast array of umbrellas and walking sticks are displayed both in the window and along the walls. They range from ladies antique parasols to huge plain country umbrellas as well as the rare solid snakeskin wood handled umbrella which retails at an astounding £700. The choice of walking sticks is equally diverse; crook or rose knob handles, staghorn crown on hazel stick or blackthorn with silver lap-band are the decisions facing potential purchasers. Each piece is superbly crafted and this reputation for quality has meant that at least three prime ministers are amongst Smith and Sons celebrated customers; William Gladstone, Bonar Law and Lord Curzon.

They would have been served by some of the original James Smith's descendants; Smith and Son still prides itself on its as yet unbroken family tradition.

ADDRESS Hazlewood House, 53 New Oxford Street, London WC1 (020 7836 4731)
OPEN Monday to Friday, 9.30–17.25; Saturday, 10.00–17.25
UNDERGROUND Tottenham Court Road

Space NK Apothecary

Space NK Apothecary is an example of a simple idea developed – with a little perseverance, hard work and dedication – into a phenomenally successful chain of stores, one of which will – no doubt soon – be coming to a location near you.

Less than ten years ago Space NK Apothecary was simply Space NK, a stylish shop in Covent Garden's trendy (but vaguely suburban) Thomas Neal's shopping mall that sold fashionable clothing (Fenn, Wright and Mason among other labels), bags (Herve Chapelier, Osprey), and jewellery, with a corner of the store dedicated to Shu Uemera make-up products and brushes. But within two years founder Nicky Kinnaird (the NK in Space NK), decided that this minor section would be the way forward for her store. She relocated to a smaller premises on the opposite side of Thomas Neal's (Shu Uemera still operates independently from her original ground-level space while a micro-brewery has opened up in her former basement), rethought, renamed and restocked the entire store and now has a rapidly expanding chain on her hands.

The beauty of Space NK Apothecary is its beauty products. Kinnaird had been inspired by drugstores in America and Europe that stocked ranges never previously seen, smelt or smeared on in the UK. She chose carefully and began importing now-popular brands such as Philosophy, Aveda and Kiehls. She was one of the try-and-test pioneers in England, encouraging customers to sample and smell, where before they had only been allowed to look without touching. A loyal clientele soon built up.

Kinnaird lost Aveda and replaced it with entirely new ranges of products from France and the USA. Talika (who claim to have a product that helps eyelashes to grow), Jurlique (whose creams and fresheners smell better than a flower garden in full bloom), and Nuxe (richly effective body

creams and oils), alongside a fantastic range of make-up from Stila, Nars, Laura Mercier and Chantecaille mean that customers can spend inordinate amounts of time perusing Kinnaird's counters.

Space NK Apothecary has more than ten stores in the UK and is opening new branches. Kinnaird remains in touch with the needs of her customers and tries to bring them new lines from abroad. In her own words, she really has created 'a sweetshop for adults'.

ADDRESS 4 Thomas Neal's, 37 Earlham Street, London WC2 (020 7379 7030)
OPEN Monday to Saturday, 10.00–19.00; Thursday, 10.00–19.30; Sunday, 12.00–17.00
UNDERGROUND Covent Garden

Tom Tom

This is the post-war art, furniture, design and pop shop where many of London's design-shop buyers come to purchase their stock. Tom Tom is owned by Tommy Roberts, a man at least partly responsible for the interest in post-war design that has grown over the past 20 years.

But Roberts has been in this business for considerably longer. He opened a shop called Kleptomania in the late 1960s and has been trading in modernist pieces ever since. Kleptomania became Mr Freedom which was unique for its time, selling greasy café food alongside clothing. In 1972 Roberts moved the store to a large loft space with a gold-flecked floor and renamed it City Lights Studio. (Malcolm McLaren took over his former premises and was constantly being asked the whereabouts of Roberts' new place.) Only 18 months later he had moved on again, this time in the guise of Practical Styling which sold the chrome and matt-black furniture so emblematic of the 1980s.

Roberts closed that shop in 1986 and in 1993 came to rest with Tom Tom. Carpets by Pierre Cardin, Verner Panton lamps, Charles Eames chairs and tables and 1950s Knoll chairs are standard pieces passing through the tiny, two-storey premises tucked away near Centre Point. Collectors, designers, art directors and stylists – as well as other shops – come to Tom Tom to request specific pieces which Roberts will endeavour to procure through buyers located throughout Europe and the USA.

Tom Tom may be located in a tiny space, but do not be fooled, the business is huge.

ADDRESS 42 New Compton Street, London WC2 (020 7240 7909)
OPEN Tuesday to Friday, 12.00–19.00; Saturday, 11.00–18.00
UNDERGROUND Tottenham Court Road

islington

Coexistence

More than 25 years ago Mary Wiggin and Ross Bull founded what has proved to be a pioneering company, bringing awareness of design to consumers.

On 1 May 1974 Coexistence opened in Bath. Its mission was to promote contemporary design in the UK. The partners shared an enthusiasm for art and design. Wiggin's stemmed from her family business – manufacturing stainless-steel tableware and all the consequential design connections that came with that. Bull worked as an international development economist between 1979 and 1990, but he had spent much of his childhood at the Tate Gallery with his father and became interested in the work of Giocametti and Modigliani. Together the couple developed an interest in design culture by visiting college shows and craft exhibitions at the Victoria & Albert Museum.

Coexistence's inaugural stock came from Italy, France and Scandinavia as well as the UK. Several pieces were commissioned from John Makepeace, Jane and Charles Dillon, Liz Fritsch and Betty Barnden. By 1978 the couple decided to move Coexistence to Floral Street in London and for a time they kept both outlets going. When the strain of travelling proved too much the whole business moved to the capital.

Yet, as in Bath, Bull and Wiggin continued to blur the boundaries between shop and home, life and work. Dinner parties attended both by friends and colleagues in the design world gave visitors the chance to try the stock as they sat on it around the table. The wine, food and conversation that flowed were pivotal in the careers of, among others, Jasper Morrison and James Dyson.

Via a couple of other moves and a financial crisis (when the UK contract-furniture market crashed in the early 1990s), Coexistence has settled into two by-appointment-only venues, one on Upper Street and

Coexistence

the other (Coexistence Art) on Canonbury Lane just around the corner. From here Coexistence focuses on contract work – it has been responsible for supplying pieces for the interiors of Harvey Nichol's Oxo Tower Restaurant, Virgin's Club lounge in Hong Kong's Chep Lap Kok airport and an installation at Cambridge's Trinity College.

ADDRESS 288 Upper Street, London N1 (020 7354 8817)
WEBSITE www.coexistence.co.uk
OPEN by appointment only
UNDERGROUND Angel

Get Stuffed

Fabulously appropriate, Get Stuffed is the name of a taxidermy shop. The shop itself is stuffed with an incredible range of dead animals. Robert Sinclair, the owner, claims innocence in regard to the origin of some of the rarer animals that find their way into the store that he inherited from his father, and refuses to answer the questions of journalists.

ADDRESS 105 Essex Road, London N1 (020 7226 1364)
OPEN Monday to Friday, 13.00–17.00; Saturday, 13.00–15.00
UNDERGROUND Highbury and Islington

twentytwentyone

In 1993 Simon Alderson and Tony Cunningham formed a partnership called Twentieth Century Design to source and sell original modern furniture, lighting and industrial design from a converted stable building in Camden. In 1996 a shop was opened in Islington which remains today as a showroom for European, American, and Scandinavian period original design. The shop also hosts occasional events such as the exhibition of work by Charles and Ray Eames in May 1997 and later that year the launch of Michael Sodeau furniture.

In 1998 Alderson and Cunningham realised that two years further on they would be limiting their stock to pre-turn-of-the-millennium pieces – to avoid this they changed the name. At the same time the shop had a refit designed by Barber Osgerby and Associates. Later, new premises were taken in Clerkenwell (18c River Street, EC1), on the site of an old dairy, as furniture showroom (open to the public), warehouse and office space.

ADDRESS 274 Upper Street, London N1 (020 7288 1996)
WEBSITE www.twentytwentyone.com
OPEN Tuesday to Friday, 10.00–18.00; Saturday, 10.00–17.30
UNDERGROUND Angel

east

Antoni and Alison

Antoni and Alison were the first people to vacuum-pack T-shirts.

Antoni Burakowski and Alison Roberts met at St Martin's School of Art in 1982 when he was studying fashion and she was studying painting. Each was envious of the other's course and together they formed a design duo that has excelled at one good idea. The T-shirts come in seven styles and three or four possible colours (black, white, grey or red). Pick a T-shirt and then choose from a range of bizarre, clever slogans and designs: 'I'm a dizzy kiss on a marshmallow in a sunbeam', 'Portrait of a woman imagining herself to be Miss Hepburn as Holly Golightly in Breakfast at Tiffany's', 'There are lightbeams coming in and out of my head'.

In 1998, just ten years after their initial collaboration, they opened their shop, subtitled the 'Factory of Lights and Entertainment'. Perched on the corner of a large block, it is a sweet space, filled with the slightly eccentric cigarette purses, badges and toys that Antoni and Alison design. Illuminated with Blackpool flashing lights, the Factory is an amusingly apt reflection of their work.

They have also produced a clothes line – in addition to the T-shirts – that is now stocked in Selfridges. Yet, unique to a T, they choose not to show on the runway during Fashion Week, instead presenting a slideshow of their work to editors from the international press. Nor will they succumb to the advances of technology. Although much of their stock is sold abroad they have chosen to produce a mail-order catalogue in the form of a broadsheet rather than build a website. But then that is the charm of this pair. Long may they do it all their way.

ADDRESS 43 Rosebery Avenue, London EC1 (0207 833 2002)
OPEN Monday to Friday, 10.30–18.00; Saturday, 12.00–16.00
UNDERGROUND Farringdon

Eat My Handbag Bitch

A brilliant name for a brilliant shop run by a brilliant couple. Eat My Handbag Bitch started out as the title of a piece of art that one half of the pair created a few years ago and turned into a Christmas-card design for friends. George and George (that's George Enoch and Georgina Stead) liked the name so much that they gave it to their first shop when in opened in May 1999.

Enoch and Stead have always been obsessive people. They met when they were obsessively clubbing more than six years ago and began obsessively collecting pieces of furniture from the 1950s onwards when they started going out with one another soon after. Enoch was – and still is – an artist but Stead had come from a background in finance. When their obsessive furniture habit outgrew their living space they started to sell off pieces at antique fairs and finally found the space in the fast up-and-coming Truman Brewery that they now call their own.

As well as *de-rigeur* pieces by Verner Panton and Charles Eames, Eat My Handbag Bitch has a penchant for the work of British designers such as Robin Day and Robert Heritage. Accessories include radios from the 1960s and 1970s, vintage television sets and a growing line of jewellery.

Alongside the classics is an interesting range of art. Pieces by Enoch include the off-the-scale 'Millennium Butt Plug' and his 'Flaming Arse'. The latter is a bronze cast of his bottom that shoots a flame out of a hole cut where you'd expect. It left the shop soon after arrival because it was a fire hazard and has been returned to their home where it is used as a pencil holder.

The couple also use their space to support other young British artists. Chris Hammond showed and sold some of his Alpine Fantasies at Eat My Handbag Bitch, as have porn-stars-turned-artists Raven and Swan.

Eat My Handbag Bitch

They have also displayed work by op-artist Roy Pegram, now in his 80s.

Whichever era or design school they showcase, Enoch and Stead's eye for quality and design mean that Eat My Handbag Bitch is a meeting point of style and tongue-in-cheek humour that will appeal to design aficionados and those seeking bohemian baubles alike.

ADDRESS 6 Dray Walk, The Old Truman Brewery, 91–95 Brick Lane, London E1 (020 7375 3100)
WEBSITE www.eatmyhandbagbitch.co.uk
OPEN Monday to Sunday, 11.00–19.00; Friday 11.00–17.00; closed Tuesday except by appointment
UNDERGROUND Liverpool Street, Aldgate East

Mathmos

Calling all *Barbarella* fans. Anyone who has seen Roger Vadim's cult 1967 film will remember the Mathmos as a moving, subterranean liquid lava-like substance, undoubtedly an extremely appropriate name for the company that manufactures the original lava lamp.

Yet the name did not come with the company. The lava lamp was invented by Edward Craven Walker in 1963 after ten years of refining a formula that uses just wax and water. At the time, Craven Walker supported his family by running an international hospitality agency as well as pursuing his other hobby – naturism. The lava lamp might never have been invented if it had not been for Craven Walker's love of nudity. His film, *Travelling Light*, made with some friends one summer in Corsica, became the first certificated movie to show nudity in British cinemas and some of the profits funded the lava-lamp project. By the end of the 1960s the lamps were bringing in enough money for Craven Walker to found his own naturist resort, the Bournemouth and District Outdoor Club. For the next decade both businesses thrived but then in the 1970s two children died sniffing a lamp made with solvents. Although it was not one of Craven Walker's lamps (his are absolutely harmless), the bad publicity forced him to lay off more than 100 workers and lava lamps retreated from the domain of cool.

It was in this condition that Cressida Granger and David Mulley found the company in 1989. Both had been running stalls at Camden Market and Granger's success in shifting the lamps made her want to be more involved in their manufacture. They renamed, restyled and rebuilt the image of the lava lamp and have created a product whose popularity seems to know no bounds.

While the lamps are still manufactured in the countryside, the Mathmos headquarters and shop-cum-showroom are worth seeing.

Mathmos

Blobbing lamps line the walls and the store design is futuristic. This former warehouse has been transformed by HM2 architects Andrew Hanson and Richard Webb into a stylised lightbox, with each of the five floors distinguished with a bold colour. You can only visit the showroom on the ground floor, but at night the whole Grade II-listed building can be viewed, shining, from the street.

Mathmos had opened another shop at 179 Drury Lane, WC2 (now closed), and this site featured images from their design team. Hip characters such as 'Mathmos Man' and 'Collectable Collette' have been used to give distictive character identity to the lamps and increase their attractiveness.

The range is no longer limited to lava lamps. Ross Lovegrove has collaborated on a new design and Faze 3 lamps which change colour as they respond to sounds and music are part of the Mathmos catalogue. All the products are available via their fun-filled character-conscious website.

ADDRESS 20–24 Old Street, London EC1 (020 7549 2710)
WEBSITE www.mathmos.co.uk
HOURS Monday to Friday, 10.00–18.00
UNDERGROUND Old Street

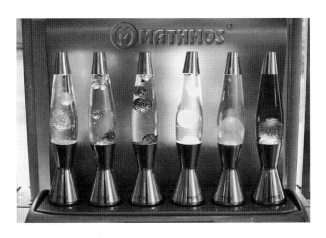

SCP

SCP is Sheridan Coakley Products. Coakley opened his first shop in Notting Hill in 1980. At that time he was starting to produce re-editions of Pel furniture from the 1930s as well as importing Italian re-editions of pieces by Mies van der Rohe and Le Corbusier. In 1985 Coakley visited Paris and was excited to discover contemporary design by Philippe Starck; he became the first UK importer of Starck furniture. He simultaneously organised the first Starck exhibition in the UK and launched the international careers of British designers Jasper Morrison and Matthew Hilton by showcasing their work at the Milan Furniture Fair.

That same year saw Coakley move to his current space on Curtain Road, at that time a convenient location – close to the metal-platers who made his re-editions – rather than a fashionable one.

Yet it is the wave of fashion sweeping round Shoreditch that turned SCP from a furniture manufacturer into the retailer it is today. Popular demand led Coakley to convert the space from a limited collection of furniture to an array of lighting, home accessories and modern furniture in autumn 1998.

The shop represents Coakley's professional history and the people he has admired, worked with and whose careers he has developed. Work by Hilton and Morrison, as well as Terence Woodgate and Konstantin Grcic, is available at the showroom. So too is lighting by Flos, Michael Sodeau and Fontana Arte. This stuff isn't cheap but, as Coakley points out, the furniture is made to last and the designs he sells are conceptual enough to not go out of fashion.

ADDRESS 135–139 Curtain Road, London EC2 (020 7739 1869)
OPEN Monday to Saturday, 9.30–18.00
UNDERGROUND Old Street

Sh!

Sh!: don't tell anyone! But Sh! has changed the face of erotic shopping. Not wanting to be leered at by greasy men, many women avoid entering shops that stock sex paraphernalia alongside shelves of pornographic magazines and videos. Ky Hoyle wanted to create a space in which women would feel comfortable and figured that the best way to do this would be to get rid of the men. Well-behaved men are allowed in, but only if they are accompanied by women. This means that Sh! gets a few couples coming in but most customers are women browsing through the stock. Not surprisingly, Sh! is popular with lesbians as well as heterosexual chicks.

At Sh!, you will see vibrators and dildos in every size, colour and shape imaginable and then some (some being the rotating, vibrating angel-headed variety). There are lingerie sets with holes cut out for nipple and fanny exposure. They come in lace or leather or rubber or good old cotton. There are stockings and suspenders and corsets and dresses. And for the slightly more daring there are whips and crops, collars, harnesses and handcuffs. Chain is sold by the metre. Harnesses allow you to hang from the ceiling while you play.

The bedroom toys and clothes are spread out over this two-floor space alongside books and magazines and amusing gifts. Sh! also stands out from most of London's other sex shops because it is located inconspicuously off Hoxton Square rather than among the neon porn shops of Soho. And when customers experience the friendly and unintrusive atmosphere of Sh! they are unlikely to return to the seedy Soho equivalent.

But remember, it's a secret, so Sh!

ADDRESS 39 Coronet Street, London N1 (020 7613 5458)
OPEN Monday to Saturday, 11.30–18.30; Thursda,y 11.30–20.00
UNDERGROUND Old Street

Viaduct

A viaduct is a many-pillared bridge. Viaduct – a 1930s galleried industrial shop space – bridges the gap between designers, architects and lovers of fine furniture. As the United Kingdom's representative for design houses such as Italian Driade and MDF, Dutch Montis, XO, Maarten van Severen and Pallucco/Bellato, Viaduct oversees an incredible trade between the design and installation fields.

Started ten years ago by James Mair, Viaduct was originally a trade showroom where specific pieces were bought for specific commissions by interior designers and architects. Although trade sales continue to make up most of Viaduct's business, the boom in the design world over the past few years has brought in an ever-increasing number of design worshippers who buy pieces for their own homes. As the customer profile changed, so too did Mair's location. Viaduct, originally in Kentish Town, moved more than five years ago to Clerkenwell, an area which has since become identified with design. Mair's architectural background meant that he could manipulate the space himself, but he brought in Harper Mackay to build the mezzanine that attractively divides the shop.

Well lit by large windows, the ground-level area houses chairs by Philippe Starck for XO and Driade (including his new Toy design which retails at an attractively low £54, a price that is expected to come down even further), Ross Lovegrove's Spin and Bluebell chairs for Driade and the fantastically plush leather range from Montis. The space underneath the mezzanine is dedicated to lighting; a variety of Pallucco and Artimede lamps are on display alongside classics such as Rodolfo Dordoni's bright Orbital Terra for Foscarini, Jasper Morrison's Global Globe light for Flos and Ingo Maurer's innovative dove lights.

Tables, chairs, storage units and sofas take up the rest of the floor space, apart from the sales office which covers two-thirds of the upper level.

Viaduct

Scattered throughout are accessories that include crockery made by Sebastian Bergne for Driade, and dumbbells by Philippe Starck that are used as door-stops in Ian Shreager's new Sanderson Hotel in Berners Street, W1.

In fact what you see at Viaduct is only the tip of the iceberg. Much of the stock, which includes entire kitchen units, is kept in storage and they often order straight from the manufacturers. The scale of the work with which they are involved means that the Summer's Street space is merely a showroom and a place to sit and discuss catalogues. Mair also likes to use it as a space for exhibitions and has supported young designers such as Tranglass (who work with recycled glass bottles), Mark Bond (who has designed furniture for Habitat), and Caterina Fadda (designer of a revolutionary pebble glass light that uses a bicycle-lamp bulb) by showing their work. At the opposite end of the reputation spectrum, Ron Arad, Tom Dixon, Danny Lane and Maarten van Severin have also had shows at Viaduct.

Even if you've never visited the shop, chances are you may have seen some of Viaduct's work. They were responsible for providing furniture for the gigantic Bluewater mall in Kent and the café in Top Shop at Oxford Circus.

ADDRESS 1–10 Summer's Street, London EC1 (020 7278 8456)
WEBSITE www.viaduct.co.uk
OPEN Monday to Friday, 9.30–18.00; Saturday, 10.30–16.00
TUBE Farringdon

oxo tower wharf

Oxo Tower Wharf

Originally built at the end of the nineteenth century as a power station to supply electricity to the Post Office, Oxo Tower Wharf only took on its current name in the 1980s when it was purchased by Coin Street Community Builders, a not-for-profit public service formed by local residents. However, it was in the 1920s that the Liebig Extract of Meat Company took possession. It demolished most of the building but maintained and extended its riverside frontage. The Liebig Extract of Meat Company was the maker of the OXO stock cube. Its architect, Albert Moore, proposed to spell the name out in electric lights on a tower but was refused permission because it would be perceived as mass advertising. He came back with 'OXO' incorporated as the windows in 'an elemental geometric form' on all four sides of the tower that now shine out from the Wharf as a London landmark. For many years it was used for cold storage, processing and packing. Meat was delivered by barge, off-loaded by large cranes fixed to the building and passed through bays (which remain on the riverside).

The building subsequently became part of the vast Vestey family butchery empire but by the early 1970s had become derelict, apart from the production of 'long eggs' for insertion into meat pies. Lord Vestey also used barges moored on the Thames outside the Wharf as helicopter landing pads. In 1984 the site came into the hands of the Coin Street Community Builders. Among other projects, they decided to undertake the huge task of refurbishment even though English Heritage refused to recommend the building for listing – most developers would have knocked it down.

Funding for the £20 million refurbishment came from the Housing Corporation, English Partnerships, private borrowing and Coin Street's own equity. Within years, Oxo Tower Wharf had won the Royal Fine Arts

Commission/BskyB Building of the Year Regeneration Award and a Royal Institute of British Architects Regional Award.

Since opening to the public in September 1996 Oxo Tower Wharf has attracted a huge number of visitors to the development and the surrounding areas. Its rooftop restaurant has been leased to Harvey Nichols and has proven especially popular thanks to its magnificent view over London's skyline from the eighth floor (the view can also be seen from the public gallery, located between the restaurant and brasserie and open daily until 22.00). Floors three through seven are divided into 78 one-, two- and three-bedroom low-rent housing association apartments.

It is below all of this that the 33 design studios are located – 11 retail studios on the second floor and 22 more on the first and ground floors. The idea behind these was to open them to designers in the community spirit that comprises the Oxo Tower Wharf development. The Coin Street Community Builders wanted to promote contemporary design by inviting young talent to use the work/retail spaces. Located in close proximity to one another, they hoped to enhance the overall effect of a creative hotspot within the Wharf. Affordable rents are maintained to encourage creative designers to these attractive sites and they have to maintain both design studio and retail elements in their space.

This has brought some very inspiring talent into the building. **Bodo Sperlein**'s award-winning ceramics are designed and sold on the first floor. His organically shaped bowls and cups are manufactured off-site, but his studio is located within the Wharf building. Italian-born and Royal College of Art-educated **Caterina Fadda** is another of the Wharf's rising stars. Her curved plates and innovative salt and pepper shakers, which nestle together resembling candles and soaps rather than ceramic pieces, have proved incredibly popular and will soon be mass-produced. She has

recently started to design lights and tables and these are also appearing regularly in lifestyle magazines all over the world.

The studios have proven very appealing to weavers of rugs and textiles as well. **Archipelago** moved their loom into their studios and the entire design, manufacture and retail process takes place from this space. So too did **Anne Selim** who weaves scarves, curtains and cushions. **Little + Collins** rugs are designed on site but their size demands that they be made elsewhere. **Salt**, who won the 1999 Ergonom award for their bespoke blinds and installation textiles, are located on the first floor. Lighting designers such as **Richard Hinton** – who is responsible for colourful fluffy feather lights that rock on springs attached to webbed-feet stands – and **plus*** (Cath Carroll and Karen Smith also make furniture, tableware and wall hangings) have also found homes in the building. Fashion designers (**Pauline Burrows**), jewellery craftsmen (**D'Argent Gallery**, **Karen Gledhill**, **Alan Vallis**), and even a holographic studio are making use of the Oxo Tower Wharf. Martin Richardson's Holographic Image Studio (**T.H.I.S**), was responsible for a David Bowie limited-edition CD cover for which Bowie modelled on-site.

While the Oxo Tower Restaurant has become a popular place to dine, filling the studio spaces has been a slower process. However, with the recent opening of the Tate Modern, located only a few minutes away on Bankside, the designers are now well placed to attract the art and design lovers who will be walking by these riverside studios.

ADDRESS Bargehouse Street, London SE1 (information 020 7401 2255) OPEN Tuesday to Sunday, 11.00–18.00; may vary slightly with each studio
UNDERGROUND Waterloo/Blackfriars/Southwark

index

Index

shop london: a guide

Index